AF761806

Emma Goldman's No-Conscription League and the First Amendment

Emma Goldman's Supreme Court appeal occurred during a transitional point for First Amendment law, as justices began incorporating arguments related to free expression into decisions on espionage and sedition cases. This book analyzes the communications that led to her arrest—writings in *Mother Earth*, a mass-mailed manifesto, and speeches related to compulsory military service during World War I—as well as the ensuing legal proceedings and media coverage. The authors place Goldman's Supreme Court appeal in the context of the more famous Schenck and Abrams trials to demonstrate her place in First Amendment history while providing insight into wartime censorship and the attitude of the mainstream press toward radical speech.

Erika J. Pribanic-Smith is an associate professor of journalism at the University of Texas at Arlington. She specializes in research examining political communication in newspapers and magazines of the nineteenth and early twentieth centuries. Specifically, she focuses on political partisanship in the press as well as the use of editorials and letters to the editor to disseminate political ideology. A former president of the American Journalism Historians Association, Pribanic-Smith has published her research in journals such as *American Periodicals*, *American Journalism*, *Journalism History*, *Kansas History*, and *Media History Monographs*. She is also the author of several book chapters.

Jared Schroeder is an assistant professor of journalism at Southern Methodist University. His research focuses on how we should interpret the First Amendment, particularly in regard to the Supreme Court's use of the marketplace of ideas theory and the changing technological landscape. In particular, his research has focused on discourse in virtual spaces and the growing roles that artificially intelligent communicators are playing in influencing the ideas that citizens encounter, comment upon, and share online. He is the author of *The Press Clause and Digital Technology's Fourth Wave* (Routledge, 2018) as well as articles in journals such as *Communication Law & Policy*, *The Review of Higher Education*, *First Amendment Studies*, and the *Journal of Media Law & Ethics*.

Emma Goldman's No-Conscription League and the First Amendment

Erika J. Pribanic-Smith and
Jared Schroeder

Routledge
Taylor & Francis Group
NEW YORK AND LONDON

First published 2019
by Routledge
52 Vanderbilt Avenue, New York, NY 10017

and by Routledge
2 Park Square, Milton Park, Abingdon, Oxon, OX14 4RN

Routledge is an imprint of the Taylor & Francis Group, an informa business

© 2019 Taylor & Francis

The right of Erika J. Pribanic-Smith and Jared Schroeder to be identified as authors of this work has been asserted by them in accordance with sections 77 and 78 of the Copyright, Designs and Patents Act 1988.

All rights reserved. No part of this book may be reprinted or reproduced or utilized in any form or by any electronic, mechanical, or other means, now known or hereafter invented, including photocopying and recording, or in any information storage or retrieval system, without permission in writing from the publishers.

Trademark notice: Product or corporate names may be trademarks or registered trademarks, and are used only for identification and explanation without intent to infringe.

Library of Congress Cataloging-in-Publication Data
A catalog record for this title has been requested

ISBN: 978-1-138-49347-6 (hbk)
ISBN: 978-1-351-02798-4 (ebk)

Typeset in Times New Roman
by Out of House Publishing

Contents

Illustrations

1 Introduction

Eight men arrived at the New York office of *Mother Earth* magazine on June 15, 1917: U.S. Marshal Thomas McCarthy, Assistant U.S. Attorney E. M. Stanton, deputy marshals, special agents, and a bomb squad. In the second-floor office, the men found portraits of editor Emma Goldman and other anarchists, book shelves lined with neatly arranged anarchist books and pamphlets, and stacked copies of the July *Mother Earth,* ready for mailing on the floor. They did not find Goldman.[1]

After a moment, she descended from the third-floor office of *The Blast* magazine, edited by her lifelong companion Alexander Berkman. Goldman—whom a visitor once described as a "severe but warm-hearted school teacher"—wore round, wire-rimmed glasses, her brown hair wound in a tight bun.[2] Newspapers frequently noted her plump frame.[3] She responded to McCarthy's notice of an arrest warrant by casually calling up the stairs to Berkman, "Some visitors are here to arrest us," and going into her bedroom to change from her rumpled work clothes.[4] The New York *Sun* reported that when McCarthy walked Goldman to the vehicles waiting downstairs, she wore a crisp white shirt, a purple skirt with matching jacket, and "a straw hat with a gay band."[5] Goldman was unperturbed—after all, she'd been arrested multiple times for anarchist sentiments published in *Mother Earth* and uttered in public speeches, and she typically was back at it in no time.[6]

But this time was different. At the height of anti-immigrant, anti-radical war hysteria, Goldman was charged with conspiracy to defeat the draft, sentenced to two years in prison, fined $10,000, and, ultimately, deported. Within weeks of her arrest, *Mother Earth* suspended, falling prey to the postal restrictions of the 1917 Espionage Act. Furthermore, McCarthy's men seized everything in the *Mother Earth* offices—back issues, checkbooks, correspondence, manuscripts, and, importantly, subscription lists to be used for tracking down other radicals.[7] As she had every other time she faced adversity, Goldman used her conspiracy trial and subsequent deportation hearing as forums to promote her anarchist ideals, including beliefs in unrestrained speech. "The free expression of the hopes and aspirations of a people is the greatest and only safety in a sane society," she contended. "In truth, it is such free expression and discussion alone that can point the most beneficial path for human progress and development."[8] The courts were unsympathetic. She left the United States in 1919 from the same city where she had arrived, departing Ellis Island on a steamer with more than 200 others that the U.S. government evicted during the first Red Scare.

Goldman's free speech struggles came just as the nation, and the court system, were becoming concerned about freedom of expression. Her federal court conviction in 1917 and the Supreme Court's decision not to hear her case the following January marked the last major instance when justices turned a blind eye to freedom of expression concerns. In fact, Goldman's friend and attorney, Harry Weinberger, was juggling her deportation case at the same time he was defending another famous anarchist, Jacob Abrams. A week before Goldman appeared before immigration officials, Weinberger had argued on Abrams's behalf before the Supreme Court. Abrams's case resulted in Justice Oliver Wendell Holmes's famous dissent, in which he fashioned the marketplace-of-ideas interpretation of the First Amendment. Justice Holmes defended the anarchist's right to speak because it contributed to the ideas that were being discussed in society.[9] Less than a month after the Supreme Court announced its Abrams decision, Goldman was going back to Russia—just as many newspapers and public hecklers had been telling her to do for decades. It was too late for her, but Goldman's case remained in the mind of Holmes and others as they decided similar cases from that point forward.

By placing Goldman's arrest, trial, and the anti-conscription communications that led to them in the context of the era's legal environment, this book seeks to fill gaps in the literature on First Amendment scholarship and one of America's most notorious rebels. Multiple sweeping biographies have told the story of Goldman's life.[10] Scholars also have examined her rhetoric, primarily through a feminist lens.[11] They have explored her contributions to anarchist movements, and they've noted her criticism of theater and art.[12] However, *Mother Earth* has received scant attention as a focus of scholarship, although historians have labeled it the most important and influential anarchist publication of its era, if not all time, and the government considered it dangerous enough to bar its circulation.[13] Furthermore, although a journal article and an unpublished thesis have focused on Goldman's free speech fights, scholars have not explored the First Amendment implications of her legal battles.[14] Yet Goldman's Supreme Court appeal occurred during a transitional point for First Amendment law, as justices began incorporating arguments related to free expression into decisions on espionage and sedition cases. This book demonstrates Goldman's place in First Amendment history while providing insight into wartime censorship and the attitude of the mainstream press toward radical speech.

This introductory chapter isolates a moment, just before a revolution in freedom of expression jurisprudence, when Goldman captured the attention of the nation with her arguments for human liberties. It sets the stage for Goldman's free speech fights by describing the cultural and political environment in the United States during her time there, while Chapter 2 explores the legal atmosphere in which Goldman wrote and spoke. Chapter 3 reviews Goldman's influences and rise to notoriety before analyzing the communications that led to Goldman's arrest—writings in *Mother Earth*, a mass-mailed manifesto, and speeches related to compulsory military service during World War I. Chapter 4 examines the ensuing legal proceedings, largely through the prism of critical mainstream newspapers. The fifth and final chapter offers an epilogue, demonstrating Goldman's effect on free speech discussions in the American court system and the press.

Foreigners in an Unfriendly Land

Born in 1869 in the Jewish quarter of Kovno, Russia (now Kaunas, Lithuania), Goldman had a turbulent and lonely childhood; although she had multiple siblings, Goldman's father was abusive and her mother distant and detached.[15] Goldman felt more connected to her sister Helena, whom she credited with filling her childhood with "whatever joy it had."[16] Biographer Alice Wexler argued that Goldman developed a need to feed and mother other people because she never experienced that herself, yet she shied away from the forced intimacy of marriage and feared becoming dominated or dependent.[17] Hence she rebelled when her father tried to arrange her marriage at age 15, fleeing with Helena to live with their sister Lena in Rochester, NY.[18] Goldman described standing with Helena on the deck of the steamer *Elbe* as it entered New York Harbor, "the Statue of Liberty suddenly emerging from the mist." To Goldman, the statue symbolized hope, freedom, and opportunity. "She held her torch high to light the way to the free country, the asylum for the oppressed of all lands," Goldman recalled. "We, too, Helena and I, would find a place in the generous heart of America. Our spirits were high, our eyes filled with tears."[19]

Goldman soon was disappointed, coming to learn that America's promise of liberty was false.[20] Young Goldman had found the Czarist regime in Russia oppressive and identified with the Nihilists who assassinated Czar Alexander in 1881.[21] Her move to the United States offered no relief, though. She found conditions in New York even more oppressive than those in Russia, particularly the factory work she began

Figure 1.1 Goldman family photo, taken in 1883, depicts Goldman standing on the left, behind her seated sister Helena and youngest brother, Morris. Goldman's brother Herman stands between parents Taube and Abraham Goldman.

Source: New York Public Library.

on arrival. She described hard, seemingly endless days at the clothing factory, under constant surveillance and "iron discipline that forbade free movement."[22]

The treatment of immigrants disappointed her most. Goldman's arrival coincided with a wave of "new immigration" that brought droves of southern and eastern Europeans, whom Americans saw as a threat to their way of life. One million refugees from the region arrived during the 1880s alone; twenty-six million arrived between 1870 and 1920. Nearly 70 percent of the immigrants that arrived during the first decades of the twentieth century were "new immigrants."[23] Powerful anti-immigrant sentiment marked this period of new immigration, shattering the "melting pot" myth of multiple cultures coinciding peacefully.[24] According to historian Gary Gerstle, the prevailing American philosophy at the time was one of civic nationalism: a belief in the fundamental equality of all humans, inalienable rights, and democratic government. However, civic nationalism competed with the nativist philosophy that being a "true American" required common blood, skin color, and inherited fitness for self-government.[25] Although progressives and other contributionists somewhat accepted the melting pot idea and welcomed immigrant cultures, new immigrants like Goldman overwhelmingly faced prejudice from Social Darwinists who saw new immigrants as genetically less fit than Anglo-Saxons, and from nativists who feared foreigners would contaminate American traditions, ideals, and standards of living.[26] Therefore, while progressive reformers of the era made significant contributions toward bettering conditions for immigrants, foreign-born American residents more often encountered a social and political environment that escalated from hostile to repressive during Goldman's time in the United States.

Restricting Immigration

One reaction to the increasing presence of "unworthy" immigrants was a call to restrict entry of foreign-born people into the nation. Earlier in the nineteenth century, a few states had tried to regulate immigration, but despite a burst of nativist sentiment in the 1850s, the federal government made no such effort. Aside from Catholics, immigrants generally had been accepted quickly into American society.[27] Restrictionist agitation began in earnest in the late nineteenth century, including the formation of lobby groups such as the American Protective Association and Immigration Restriction League.[28] Religious discrimination and Anglo-Saxon racial superiority, invasion of the labor force, and the dangers of radicalism were among the arguments restrictionists used to "make the case for narrowing the gates."[29]

Racial and Cultural Inequality

Immigration opponents associated inequality with cultural and racial barriers separating new immigrants from Anglo-American traditions: religion (many of the new immigrants were Roman Catholic, Jewish, or Eastern Orthodox), language, and strange customs.[30] Conservative Americans believed civic nationalist values needed to be revered and defended against foreign ideas. Therefore, conservative organizations such as the Sons and Daughters of the American Revolution, National Security League, and American Legion aimed to prepare immigrants for citizenship by teaching literacy and government mechanics as well as indoctrinating them to accept patriotic rituals and a "reverential" view of American history. However, conservatives questioned the ability of new immigrants to become good American citizens due to their poor racial stock, favoring instead immigrant restriction and more stringent naturalization requirements to protect society against "dangerous foreign influences."[31]

Eugenicists similarly doubted immigrants could become American, asserting that only immigrants who could "contribute positively to the national gene pool" should be allowed to enter the country and eventually assimilate.[32] Popular books circulating at the time asserted that biological differences between Anglo-Saxon Protestants and "lesser" races were unchangeable. Southern and eastern European immigrants fell below Anglo-Saxons in the racial hierarchy, with Asians and Africans ranking even lower.[33] Even President Theodore Roosevelt, who eventually became the Progressive Party's leader, promoted the idea of an American "race" as "the greatest English-speaking race"—a higher, civilized race that would triumph over the "savage" ones. He considered new immigrants to be lacking in "the racial makeup necessary to succeed in America."[34] Thus, many Anglo-Americans became confident in the superiority of their own race and culture and increasingly felt threatened by the growing presence of foreigners that they deemed inferior.[35]

Labor and Restriction

Just as some argued that the presence of new immigrants corroded American culture, others asserted that the influx of foreigners into the workplace degraded the American labor force and, by extension, the living conditions of the working class. Somewhat ironically, the United States's rapid industrialization at the turn of the century created a dependence on imported workers. Between 1870 and 1910, the American labor force transformed from mostly agrarian to overwhelmingly manufacturing.[36] Industrial technology changed the nature of labor, "deskilling" work that skilled craftsmen previously performed.[37] Whereas the "old" northern and western European immigrants seldom worked in unskilled positions, a majority of new immigrants—including women and children—filled unskilled and semi-skilled occupations. This division contributed to the perception that new immigrants were more "foreign" than old immigrants. It also created a social division between new immigrants and both old immigrants and native-born Americans, as the new immigrants were confined to the bottom rungs of the occupational hierarchy in the most difficult, dirty, and dangerous jobs, unable to escape or move upward.[38] New immigrants in unskilled and semi-skilled positions toiled in conditions that could be described as oppressive and unhealthy at best, deadly at worst. Furthermore, in addition to making lower wages than their native-born counterparts, new immigrants and their families received significantly lower pay-outs if they were injured or killed on the job.[39]

Figure 1.2 This 1905 postcard depicts Hester Street in New York's "Jewish Quarter," the Lower East Side of Manhattan. Goldman gravitated to this impoverished area when she first moved to New York City because of its radical activity.

Source: New York Public Library.

The immigrant woman came to be viewed as an even lower class than the immigrant man. Although independence was a prerequisite for citizenship under the tenets of civic nationalism, dependence on a husband or father characterized "proper womanhood." Thus, independent women like Goldman were perceived as destabilizing to the social order.[40] Some working women (both native and immigrant) were motivated as much by economic need as a spirit of emancipation. However, poverty forced many single and unmarried immigrant women into the workforce, and one-fourth of the five million women working for wages in the Progressive Era filled manufacturing jobs. First- and second-generation immigrant women supplied a majority of the workforce in garment factories—where Goldman found her first jobs in the United States—as well as cotton mills, canning plants, and commercial laundries. Regardless of the position, women earned far less pay than their male counterparts.[41]

Low pay and social isolation placed new immigrants in strikingly different living conditions from many native-born Americans. Samuel Gompers, head of the American Federation of Labor, argued in favor of immigrant restriction because whole communities had "witnessed a rapid deterioration in the mode of living of their working classes consequent on the incoming of the swarms of lifelong poverty-stricken aliens."[42] The tenements in New York City's Lower East Side, where Goldman first resided upon moving to the city, were representative of working-class living conditions in many urban areas: 39 tenements housed 2,871 people with no baths, limited access to running water, and one of the highest mortality rates in the world from a variety of diseases.[43] Because immigrants clustered together in the working class areas of industrial cities, nativists viewed such tenements as ethnic "ghettos" and associated immigrants with poverty, illness, and other urban problems.[44] Therefore, while the influx of new immigrant laborers allowed the United States to emerge as an industrial power, generating wealth for a small portion of the American population, they also became the symbol of what historian Matthew Jacobson called the "ugliest features of corporate capitalism amid rapid industrialization—its exploitive wages, its inhuman hours, its physical dangers, its degradations."[45]

Immigrants and Radicalism

New immigrants also came to be seen as the face of radicalism. The popularity of Socialism and anarchism in Europe during the late nineteenth century caused some Americans to fear that "radical immigrants would disrupt the American way of life."[46] Though most foreign-born Americans were not inherently radical, the discrimination they experienced living in America pushed several immigrants leftward. The rift between native-born and foreign-born Americans grew as the latter became increasingly associated with class warfare and labor disputes—disputes that historian Vivian Gornick asserted were intended not to destroy American systems but to participate in them.[47]

Low wages, long hours, and unsafe conditions generated dissatisfaction among the labor force at the turn of the century.[48] National labor organizations formed to fight for improvements, in some cases instilling socialist and anarchist ideas in sectors of the working class. Although these organizations encompassed both native- and foreign-born workers, unionization helped new immigrants "challenge presumptions about their isolation and passivity."[49] Through unions and on their own, approximately seven million workers participated in more than 36,000 strikes during the decades around the turn of the century.[50] Heavy new immigrant participation in strikes reflected their domination of the work force in most industries, but anticommunists perceived that foreign workers were "vulnerable to radical propaganda in ways that American workers were not" because of their unfamiliarity with English, illiteracy, and isolation from American cultural influences. Eventually, nativists assumed all strikes to be immigrant-instigated and un-American.[51] According to Jacobson, labor agitation throughout the era "conjured images of blood in the streets, an explosive and distinctly *foreign* brand of political chaos," which "seemed to prove the folly of accepting the world's 'dangerous classes' as a chief import."[52]

Labor historian Thomas Mackaman distinguished between labor militancy—including local labor struggles such as strikes, marches, and run-ins with authorities—and radicalism, which he tied to national and community parties that "sought to articulate what they perceived to be the class interests of workers."[53] In addition to the Socialist Party, labor radicalism included the Industrial Workers of the World (IWW, known colloquially as Wobblies). Founded in 1905 by exploited miners, lumberjacks, and migrant field hands of the west, the IWW believed in syndicalism, a foreign labor movement that emphasized the takeover of industries by autonomous worker unions or syndicates.[54]

Radicalism was not confined to labor disaffection, though. New York's largely Jewish Lower East Side became a center of radical activity in the early twentieth century. As Gornick described it: "The tenements, the streets, the life itself were choked with noise, dirt, and poverty… Here, during these years, a whole Yiddish-speaking world had been brought to life."[55] After Finns, Yiddish-speaking Jews like Goldman comprised the second largest and most prominent radical community in the country. An influx of Jewish immigrants arrived early in the twentieth century who had been exposed to old-world socialism due to persecution in Russia, Latvia, and Lithuania.[56] Radical speeches rang out day and night in lecture halls and mass meetings as well as on street corners and in parks.[57] The most prolific of the radicals, anarchists centered philosophically around distrust of centralized power and belief that governments repressed individual liberty while stifling intellectual and artistic creativity.[58] Regardless of the type of radicalism immigrants practiced, their views threatened the idea of civic nationalism.[59]

Roosevelt's Anti-Immigrant Laws

The association between radicalism and new immigrants influenced legislation at the turn of the century. As Jacobson explained, "threats posed by immigration were threats to national sovereignty, and therefore the state held the same rights and duties to curb this foreign menace as it did to protect its citizens in times of war."[60] Legislative restriction began in the 1880s with the Chinese Exclusion Act, which barred Chinese immigrant laborers from entering the country and prevented Chinese immigrants already residing in the United States from becoming citizens. Eugenicists considered Asians to be even lower on the racial hierarchy than southern and eastern Europeans, and their strange ways seemed to some an even bigger threat to American culture. Instigated by concerns that Chinese workers accepted very low wages and undercut living standards, the Chinese Exclusion Act aimed to ensure that the Chinese population would not grow enough to threaten democracy.[61] This discriminatory law set the stage for broader restrictions of immigration, which included new immigrants and especially radicals from Europe.

Roosevelt believed immigrants needed to be Americanized to accept and practice political and religious ideas, language, and other American customs, leaving behind their own cultural icons and practices. However, with limited ability to enact Americanization policies, Roosevelt worked to control immigration and naturalization.[62] Roosevelt supported efforts to exclude prospective immigrants who lacked the ability and will to Americanize. One such effort was the Immigration Act of 1903, also known as the Anarchist Exclusion Act.[63] Labor strikes of the 1880s first brought widespread attention to anarchist ideas. An anarchist's assassination of President William McKinley in 1901—for which Goldman was arrested as an alleged conspirator—solidified fears that anarchism posed a danger to American society. In his first address to Congress after succeeding the late McKinley, Roosevelt proclaimed that anarchists and "those like them should be kept out of this country, and if found here they should be promptly deported to the country whence they came."[64] The 1903 act barred entry into the United States for "anarchists, or persons who believe in or advocate the overthrow by force or violence of the Government of the United States."[65] Although few were excluded or deported for purported anarchism under the 1903 act, Jacobson argued that these laws created a precedent for exporting "discontent through a

Figure 1.3 A *Puck* cartoon titled "The 'Reds' and the 'Yellows'" blamed anarchists and sensational newspapers for the assassination of President William McKinley.

Source: Library of Congress.

machinery of repressive speech codes, unforgiving alien laws, and ever-vigilant government bureaucracies."[66]

In 1907, Roosevelt signed an amendment to the 1903 act, barring entry to the United States for the mentally ill, carriers of infectious diseases, paupers, contract laborers, and unaccompanied minors. It also expanded the definition of anarchism to include anyone who advocated the overthrow not only of the U.S. government but of all government, "or of all forms of law, or the assassination of public officials."[67] Officials attempted to deport Goldman under this act in November 1907, after she re-entered the country from a lecture trip abroad, but they were unsuccessful. Though an investigation demonstrated irrefutably that Goldman was an anarchist, officials questioned whether she was an alien under the 1907 law given her long residence in the United States and the fact that her father was a naturalized citizen.[68]

In addition to increasing restrictions on immigration, the 1907 act established the United States Immigration Commission (also known as the Dillingham Commission) to study whether certain slow-assimilating groups should have their ability to enter the U.S. curtailed or eliminated. Delivered in 1911, the commission's 41-volume report indicated that new immigrants from southern and eastern Europe were unskilled, illiterate transients living in areas of high crime and disease, correlating these issues with ethnic characteristics rather than environmental conditions. The commission recommended greater federal oversight of immigration policy, including quotas limiting immigrants of specific nationalities and the implementation of a literacy test to restrict "undesirable immigration."[69]

Progressive Americanization

As an alternative to restrictionism, progressive reformers aimed to improve the lives of immigrants. The progressive movement emerged as a response to the detriments of industrialism, especially working and living conditions of the poor. Historians note that depression conditions marked much of the late nineteenth and early twentieth centuries. A depression that stretched from 1893 to 1897 deepened poverty, increased class conflict, and raised doubts about the virtues of industrialization. It led many to question whether their belief in self-regulation was contributing to society's downfall. Furthermore, as the gap widened between rich and poor, America's promise of equal opportunity waned.[70] Progressives believed someone needed to cure the ills that the economic downturn caused. Muckraking journalists and authors such as Jacob Riis and Upton Sinclair joined the movement, publishing books and exposé articles that brought to light deplorable living and working conditions as well as government corruption.[71]

Among the most famous of these crusading writers, Lincoln Steffens was a close friend of Goldman's—he testified on her behalf at her 1917 federal court trial.[72]

Other progressive reformers lobbied for a regulatory state to intervene against corporations that prevented equal opportunity for the masses.[73] Some historians label progressivism as a middle-class movement. Situated economically between the nation's wealthy and impoverished, middle-class Americans noted that the rich and the poor lived by different sets of cultural rules that deviated from the Victorian emphasis on morals, self-control, and refinement.[74] At the same time, the middle class developed its own set of values, preferencing community over the individual. Middle-class values only served those with enough resources and stability to use them; the poor were unable to participate, including many immigrants.[75] As Gerstle noted, "grinding poverty was preventing workers, even those with full political and civil rights, from achieving economic security or the leisure necessary to cultivate their civic virtue."[76] Several strains of progressivism developed in response. Jane Addams and others specifically crusaded on behalf of the immigrant population, while others focused on different issues. Overall, however, historian Michael McGerr asserted that progressives "intended nothing less than to transform Americans, to remake the nation's feuding, polyglot population into their own middle-class image."[77]

One aspect of progressive reform called for bridging the gap between native- and foreign-born by making immigrants more American.[78] Historian Christina Ziegler-McPherson argued that progressives shared an obsession with citizenship, including both legal status and behavior; they viewed citizenship and democracy as tools to "reform the polity and economy."[79] Progressives opposed immigration restriction as discriminatory. Instead, they reacted to the turn-of-the-century surge of immigration with an Americanization movement, seeking to assimilate working-class immigrants into the culture of middle-class values and behaviors, with the hope that socioeconomic status would follow.[80] Progressive reformers argued that immigrants deserved special help because they suffered from unique disadvantages distinct from being poor or working class, including language, inexperience with urban industrial life, and unfamiliarity with American ways. These foreign residents required proper assistance to become true Americans; unsupervised assimilation could produce "the wrong kind of Americans."[81]

The Americanization movement fit perfectly into the concept of New Nationalism that Roosevelt espoused as the basis for his Progressive political philosophy in the 1910s. Though some historians have labeled Progressivism as radical, others call it conservative for its adherence to civic nationalism.[82] Though Roosevelt aimed to help working-class immigrants who properly adapted to American life, he continued to assert that he would discipline those who refused to become American. Roosevelt even welcomed "inferior" southern and eastern Europeans under his new policy so long as they assimilated and bettered themselves.[83]

Wilson's War on Germany and Hyphenated Immigrants

Hostilities overseas increased calls for Americanization, especially of immigrants from nations sparring in World War I. A Yugoslavian nationalist assassinated Austrian Archduke Franz Ferdinand in June 1914, sparking a crisis that resulted in Austria-Hungary's declaration of war on Serbia. Soon other countries entered the fray, resulting in conflict between the Allies (Russia, France, and Britain) and the Central Powers (Austria-Hungary and Germany). President Woodrow Wilson publicly urged Americans to stay neutral as "one great nation at peace"; he counseled immigrant groups to leave all other countries behind so that Americans could "get rid of the things that divide and make sure of the things that unite."[84]

Despite Wilson's calls for neutrality, the United States was in a recession, and there was money to be made by lending funds or selling goods to the warring nations. The questions of selling munitions and whether the U.S. should prepare its military for conflict became heated public debates among capitalists, militarists, and pacifists.[85] War opponents came from every background, region, and political party, all sharing a revulsion for the conflict claiming millions of lives overseas.[86] The disparate groups largely coalesced in the American Union Against Militarism (AUAM), founded in 1915 to fight against the preparedness movement. Although preparedness advocates similarly converged in organizations such as the American Defense Society and National Security League, historians argue that the pacifists had most Americans on their side until Congress declared war in April 1917.[87] However, the chances that the United States would remain impartial decreased after a German submarine sank the British ocean liner *Lusitania* in May 1915, killing more than 100 American passengers. Though many still did not support U.S. intervention in the war, public opinion became increasingly anti-German. Wilson himself began portraying Germany as a foreign enemy.[88] As anti-German sentiment spread, American nationalism increased. War opponents began to see indications that Americans would not tolerate speech they perceived as unpatriotic. For instance, New Yorkers were indignant about an exhibit by the AUAM, which some called treasonable for its portrayal of Uncle Sam as a bloodthirsty warrior.[89]

Pacifists began to question Wilson's devotion to neutrality late in the fall of 1915 when he proposed a reorganization and expansion of the army and navy, although he attempted to assure dissenters that "reasonable preparation" was not the same as militarism. The struggle over the president's proposal became the major battle in Congress during the ensuing winter, with a modified bill ultimately passing in June 1916. As he attempted to please both militarists and pacifists, Wilson signed the National Defense Act—doubling the size of the army and federalizing the National Guard—but asserted that these measures were intended to defend the homeland against potential invaders, not wage combat overseas.[90] In fact, with anti-war sentiment swelling as Allied casualties mounted overseas, Wilson ran his 1916 presidential campaign as the "peace" candidate with the slogan, "He kept us out of war." His platform also patriotically asserted "in a world on fire, only unadulterated Americanism would do." He lashed out against immigrants who remained loyal to their old countries, pushing for full assimilation as flag-waving citizens and calling "hyphenates" un-American.[91]

Wilson delivered on his promises for peace by issuing a note in December 1916 asking the belligerent powers to announce their terms to end the war and by making a speech calling for "peace without victory." Foreign powers responded that they would not concede to end a war without some victory to compensate for all their sacrifices. In fact, German Kaiser Wilhelm issued an order in January 1917 for unlimited submarine warfare "with all possible vigor." Wilson continued a middle ground, calling for armed neutrality: protecting non-military American vessels from German U-boats without entering the war. But as German submarines began sinking American vessels, Wilson broke his resolve. An April speech vowed that America would fight "for the ultimate peace of the world and for the liberation of its peoples" with no selfish ends or desire for conquest.[92] Historians have argued that Wilson saw Germany as a threat not only to Americans' safety but also their ideals, thus promoting the war as a conflict between democracy and autocracy.[93] Wilson's "othering" rhetoric filtered down to the American public. Ironically, when the AUAM sought to test America's belief in democracy by calling for a referendum to consult the people before declaring war, mainstream newspapers—assuming that U.S. intervention would secure an Allied victory—blasted the pacifist group and accused them of serving as German agents.[94]

The day after Wilson signed the declaration of war, Congress began debating the Selective Service Act. This was not the first time the United States had employed a draft system; it had done so ineffectively during the Civil War, resulting in massive resistance and multiple riots.[95] However, John Whiteclay Chambers asserted that conditions of the Progressive Era—specifically a popularly legitimated state and intensive nationalism—made World War I conscription successful.[96] Previously, Americans viewed conscription in Europe and Asia as

Figure 1.4 World War I propaganda directed at immigrants included a poster telling them, "You came here seeking freedom. You must now help to preserve it."

Source: Library of Congress.

tyrannous. A crusade to win support for conscription began as soon as the war did, often rolled into preparedness arguments. Conscription supporters framed the draft as democratic, emphasizing the relationship between citizenship rights and military obligations. As intervention became more likely, it became clear that Americans would not tolerate a permanent system of universal conscription, but most would accept a temporary, equitable selective draft in wartime.[97] Great Britain helped American conscriptionists' case by instituting a draft for the first time in the nation's history in 1916, becoming "the last of the warring nations in Europe to acknowledge that patriotism alone could not persuade enough men to replace those who had fallen."[98] Britain's act weakened the Anglo-Saxon volunteer military tradition and helped legitimate the idea of wartime conscription in America.[99]

Citing the need to raise a larger army for effective participation in the war, Congress passed the Selective Service Act on April 28, 1917; Wilson signed it into law on May 18.[100] Wilson insisted the Selective Service Act did not call for a conscription of the unwilling but rather "selection from a Nation which has volunteered in mass."[101] Nonetheless, the draft, like the war in general, sparked fierce dissent. Alienated economic groups believed the nation's poor were being condemned to die for a "Wall Street war," and the disenfranchised were skeptical about supporting a war that claimed to be on behalf of democracy.[102] Furthermore, many saw the draft as coercive. Although the act allowed religious exemptions, conscientious objectors were harassed, threatened, and in some cases arrested.[103] The AUAM created the Civil Liberties Bureau—precursor to the American Civil Liberties Union—to provide free legal advice for conscientious objectors. Its director served several months in prison for violating the Selective Service Act.[104] Furthermore, Weinberger represented the AUAM in a constitutional challenge to the conscription law, based on the Thirteenth Amendment's ban on involuntary servitude. The Supreme Court upheld the law, asserting, "Indeed, it may not be doubted that the very conception of a just government and its duty to the citizen includes the duty of the citizen to render military service in case of need, and the right of the government to compel it."[105]

Wartime Radicalism

After America's entry into the war, government and independent organizations set about catching draft dodgers and squashing anti-war dissent in general. As American fear of radicals grew, a spirit of repression increasingly replaced the progressive movement.[106] War produced an explosion of dissent, especially among the immigrant community. Mackaman asserted, "Socialists, syndicalists, and anarchists made appeals to the new immigrants condemning the war and pointing to it as a vindication of their various perspectives."[107] The Russian Revolution, six months after the U.S. entered the war, inspired further radicalism. Bolsheviks overthrew the Russian czar and seized power in the fall of 1917, supplanting capitalism with communism. Bolstered by the success of the revolution overseas, Bolshevik sympathizers in America increased their arguments against capitalism and its perils, including militarism.[108]

In the face of persistent anti-war sentiment, the government first engaged in a propaganda effort to boost support, especially among the immigrant population. Wilson aimed to rally the war's opponents around civic nationalist principles.[109] The Committee on Public Information (also known as the Creel Committee) played a significant role in shaping American attitudes toward war as well as toward immigrants, triggering a racial nationalism based on Anglo-American superiority.[110] Nationalist propaganda called for the Americanization of immigrants while demonizing difference and dissent, often labeling dissenters as German sympathizers.[111] Ziegler-McPherson asserted that Americanization became about cultural conformity as a loyalty test.[112] Anyone who refused to become a true American would be punished through censorship, jail, or deportation in what Gerstle called the largest curtailment of free expression for the sake of national security since the Alien and Sedition Acts of the 1790s.[113] In this atmosphere, the Bureau of Immigration created a special division to expedite deportation proceedings against immigrant anarchists and other radicals.[114]

Though war had stemmed the tide of immigration, it had not decreased the number of new immigrants in the workforce. The government aimed to keep immigrant workers in production behind the war effort and off the picket line.[115] However, the IWW strongly opposed the war and agitated for workers to refuse to participate in the war economy. The Californian state government recommended mass internment of immigrant workers, but the federal government decided instead to prosecute Wobblies under new anti-syndicalism laws and arrest members for disrupting the war effort.[116] Vigilantes, who had been harassing the IWW for nearly a decade, became emboldened by government anti-radical measures during the war and murdered at least one IWW organizer.[117] Members of a Bisbee, Arizona, vigilante group—deputized by the Cochise County Sheriff—illegally deported hundreds of striking IWW mine workers. This Citizens' Protective League subsequently set up a loyalty test system that either issued "passports" to town residents or deported them depending on their answers to questions about the war and the strike.[118]

In a country overtaken by patriotic, anti-immigrant, anti-radical hysteria, vigilantism was a common occurrence, often conducted in coordination with government and law enforcement. Hundreds of middle-class Americans joined groups such as the American Protective

League, the American Legion, the Ku Klux Klan, and Native Sons of the Golden West, all of which engaged in vigilante attacks and intimidation tactics against pacifists, immigrants, and radicals.[119] Once deputized by the Justice Department's Bureau of Investigation, the American Protective League's primary purpose became rounding up draft dodgers in their infamous "slacker raids." Historians argue that the APL's zealous activities fanned ethnic animosities to such an extent that mobs forced immigrants and others suspected of disloyalty to kiss the American flag, recite the Pledge of Allegiance, or sing the "Star-Spangled Banner." Those found to be insufficiently patriotic often were tarred and feathered, as Goldman's partner Ben Reitman was when the two visited San Diego to support the IWW.[120] The Justice Department conducted numerous investigations itself, often threatening its targets into silence.[121] Authorities arrested nearly 6,000 men for failure to register in the summer of 1917 alone, many of them poorer men isolated from larger society and the war effort by geography as well as economic, ethnic, or racial status. Those in urban areas often were unskilled ethnic immigrants.[122]

In this atmosphere of refusal to tolerate dissent, Congress passed a series of laws that ensured radicals would remain quiet or leave—whether willingly or by force. Gerstle called the "disciplinary project" the federal government launched in 1917 and 1918 "a draconian and racialized system of immigration restriction."[123] Wilson's first act against immigrants occurred days after the April 1917 declaration of war, when the president invoked the Alien Enemies Act. The measure first required German males age 14 and older to register and restricted their movements; it was broadened to include Austro-Hungarian males and, eventually, all female enemy aliens.[124] The Espionage and Sedition Acts, which will be discussed in more detail in Chapter 2, criminalized interference with the war effort and criticism of national institutions. Congress passed the two laws after Wilson called for them in a speech lamenting that foreign-born citizens had been allowed to pour "the poison of disloyalty into the very arteries of our national life" as well as "to bring the authority and good name of our Government into contempt, to destroy our industries wherever they thought it effective for their vindictive purposes to strike at them, and to debase our politics to the uses of foreign intrigue." Wilson urged Congress to enact laws "at the earliest possible moment" that would crush "such creatures of passion, disloyalty, and anarchy."[125]

Under the Alien Enemies Act, immigrants could be sent to internment camps, and the Espionage and Sedition Acts empowered authorities to censor, imprison, or deport immigrant radicals. Congress also passed laws during the war years that aimed to keep alien radicals out. Congress had attempted multiple times to make literacy a condition for admission and saw it vetoed by three presidents who viewed immigrants as necessary for economic development. On the eve of U.S. entry into the war, however, the Immigration Act of 1917 passed over presidential veto due to increasing support for immigration restriction. The law discriminated against certain Asian and European groups, including the predominantly Catholic and Jewish new immigrants from southern and eastern Europe, whose literacy rates were far lower than those from other European regions.[126] In the wake of the Russian Revolution—while Goldman was serving her sentence for anti-conscription activities—the 1918 Immigration Act further expanded the definition of what it meant to be an anarchist in order to "exclude and expel from the United States" all aliens that were "members of the anarchist and similar classes." The act also removed a provision from prior laws on anarchist expulsion that aliens who had resided in the United States for more than five years were not subject to deportation.[127] Though the act stripped anarchist immigrants of the right to due process, the courts did not deem the law unconstitutional because it was directed at aliens and not citizens; thus, "safeguards protecting individuals' liberty against government power" did not apply.[128]

Post-War Red Scare

Goldman, who had been in the United States for more than thirty years, was deported under the 1917 and 1918 acts. Though the war ended long before Goldman's December 1919 departure, the United States was plagued with disorder. The Bolshevik Revolution, a massive strike wave, and a rash of anarchist bombings reinforced America's fear of immigrant radicals like Goldman and launched America into its first Red Scare.[129] The war's sudden end in November 1918 caused consumer prices to skyrocket by more than 15 percent per year in 1919 and 1920, and wage loss due to inflation instigated worker unrest. Labor strikes in 1919 ultimately involved more than four million workers. Fear of repeating the Bolshevik Revolution in America justified government officials and businessmen in crushing all uprisings, supported by a public—under the residual effects of wartime propaganda—that quickly labeled any labor organizers as Communists or Bolsheviks.[130]

Even more frightening to many Americans than labor uprisings were the series of bombings carried out by followers of Italian anarchist Luigi Galleani to retaliate against government suppression of immigrants and radicals.[131] Editor of the anarchist newsletter *Cronaca Sovversiva* (Subversive Chronicle), to which Goldman contributed multiple articles, Galleani had arrived in the United States in 1901.[132] His brand of radical anarchism espoused direct, often violent actions. Though Galleanists had carried out multiple bombings since 1914, a

Figure 1.5 The home of Attorney General A. Mitchell Palmer sustained minor damage from an alleged Galleanist bomb in June 1919, but the attack had major repercussions.

Source: Library of Congress.

large concentration of them in late 1917 and early 1918 raised concerns, spurring a raid on the offices of *Cronaca Sovversiva*. Mirroring events at the *Mother Earth* offices in 1917, authorities confiscated the names and addresses of *Cronaca Sovversiva*'s subscribers, arrested its editors, and ultimately suppressed the publication.[133] Evidence collected during the raids on the *Cronaca* offices and Galleani's home led to his deportation in January 1919 for advocating the violent overthrow of government and authoring a bomb-making manual. On his way out of the country, Galleani urged his followers to seek revenge. Soon, flyers appeared threatening to show no pity against a government that had shown immigrants none: "And deport us! We will dynamite you!" In April, Galleanists carried out their pledge, sending bombs to 36 politicians and businessmen—including John D. Rockefeller and 1918 Immigration Act sponsor Thomas Hardwick.[134] Then in June, the anarchist group exploded bombs simultaneously across the country, targeting politicians who had backed anti-sedition laws and deportation as well as judges who had handed anarchists lengthy prison sentences. Attorney General A. Mitchell Palmer's home suffered damage from one of the blasts.[135] Though Goldman and Berkman were in prison at the time, investigators suspected their followers may have been responsible before blaming the Galleanists.[136]

The bombings were part of the impetus for a new anti-radical unit in the Justice Department called the General Intelligence Division, headed by J. Edgar Hoover, which aimed to root out suspected revolutionaries. After his home was attacked, Palmer ordered the Justice Department and other agencies to conduct a massive assault on American radicals. Raids conducted in the last half of 1919—including one against the Union of Russian Workers in New York City on the second anniversary of the Russian Revolution—netted several hundred alien radicals. Nearly 200 Russians apprehended during the "Palmer raids" were deported that December on the same ship as Goldman.[137] Many of the immigrants convicted and deported under the various anti-radical and immigration acts of the early twentieth century were ousted not for their actions but for their spoken and/or written rebellion against civic nationalism, though the courts did not recognize their cases to be associated with the First Amendment. The next chapter explores the legal environment during this perilous era for First Amendment rights.

Notes

1 Scene recreated from Emma Goldman, *Living My Life* (Garden City, NY: Garden City Publishing, 1934), 609–611, and "Berkman and Emma Goldman Held for Plot," *Sun* (New York), June 16, 1917.
2 Alice Wexler, *Emma Goldman: An Intimate Life* (New York: Pantheon Books, 1984), 200–201.
3 See, for example, *Indianapolis Star*, June 6, 1917; "Rioting at Anti-Draft Meeting in Bronx," *Allentown* (PA) *Democrat*, June 5, 1917.
4 Goldman, *Living My Life*, 610–611.
5 "Berkman and Goldman Held for Plot."
6 New York Police Department records list twelve total arrests between 1893 and 1917; in most of the cases she was either not charged or her case was dismissed. See Criminal Record of Emma Goldman, Bureau of Investigation, Department of Justice, in Candace Falk, with Ronald J. Zboray, et al., eds., *The Emma Goldman Papers: A Microfilm Edition* (Alexandria, VA: Chadwyck-Healey, Inc., 1990; hereafter referred to as Goldman Papers), reel 63.
7 Goldman, *Living My Life*, 612, 622, 642, 709; Emma Goldman, "Between Jails," *Mother Earth*, August 1917, 207–208; *Mother Earth Bulletin*, October 1917.
8 Goldman, *Living My Life*, 704.
9 Thomas Healy, "The Justice Who Changed His Mind: Oliver Wendell Holmes, Jr., and the Story Behind *Abrams v. United States*," *Journal of Supreme Court History* 39, 1 (2014): 35–78.
10 See, for example, Richard Drinnon, *Rebel in Paradise: A Biography of Emma Goldman* (Chicago: University of Chicago Press, 2012); Candace Falk, *Love,*

Anarchy, and Emma Goldman: A Biography (New Brunswick, NJ: Rutgers University Press, 1990); Vivian Gornick, *Emma Goldman: Revolution as a Way of Life* (New Haven, CT: Yale University Press, 2011); Theresa Moritz and Albert Moritz, *The World's Most Dangerous Woman: A New Biography of Emma Goldman* (Vancouver: Subway Books, 2002); Wexler, *Intimate Life*.

11 For gendered interpretations of Goldman's life and work, see Kathy E. Ferguson, *Emma Goldman: Political Thinking in the Streets* (Lanham, MD: Rowman & Littlefield, 2011); Bonnie Haaland, *Emma Goldman: Sexuality and the Impurity of the State* (New York: Black Rose Books, 1993); Clare Hemmings, *Considering Emma Goldman: Feminist Political Ambivalence and the Imaginative Archive* (Durham, NC: Duke University Press, 2018); Carla Hustak, "Saving Civilization from the 'Green-Eyed Monster': Emma Goldman and the Sex Reform Campaign against Jealousy, 1900–1930," *Journal of Transnational American Studies* 4, 1 (2012): 1–29; Donna M. Kowal, *Tongue of Fire: Emma Goldman, Public Womanhood, and the Sex Question* (Albany: State University of New York Press, 2016); Linda Lumsden, "Anarchy Meets Feminism: A Gender Analysis of Emma Goldman's *Mother Earth*, 1906–1917," *American Journalism* 24, 3 (2007): 31–54; Heather Ostman, "'The Most Dangerous Woman in America': Emma Goldman and the Rhetoric of Motherhood in *Living My Life*," *Prose Studies* 31, 1 (2009): 55–73; Penny A. Weiss and Loretta Kensinger, eds., *Feminist Interpretations of Emma Goldman* (University Park: Pennsylvania State University Press, 2007).

12 For discussions of Goldman's contributions to anarchy, see Keith Cassidy, "The American Left and the Problem of Leadership, 1900–1920," *South Atlantic Quarterly* 82, 4 (1983): 387–397; Marian J. Morton, *Nowhere at Home: Emma Goldman and the American Left* (New York: Twayne, 1992); Martha Solomon, *Emma Goldman* (Boston: Twayne, 1987); Martha Solomon, "Ideology as Rhetorical Constraint: The Anarchist Agitation of 'Red Emma' Goldman," *Quarterly Journal of Speech* 74, 2 (1988): 184–200; Kenneth C. Wenzer, *Anarchists Adrift: Emma Goldman and Alexander Berkman* (St. James, NY: Brandywine Press, 1996). Solomon explored dramatic criticism in a chapter of *Emma Goldman* (pp. 87–111); see also Candace Falk, "Emma Goldman: Passion, Politics, and the Theatrics of Free Expression," *Women's History Review* 11, 1 (2002): 11–26.

13 Peter Glassgold, *Anarchy! An Anthology of Emma Goldman's* Mother Earth (Berkeley, CA: Counterpoint, 2012); Claire Goldstene, *The Struggle for America's Promise: Equal Opportunity at the Dawn of Corporate Capital* (Jackson: University Press of Mississippi, 2014), 78; David Porter, *Vision on Fire: Emma Goldman on the Spanish Revolution* (Chico, CA: AK Press, 2006), 23. Lumsden's "Anarchy Meets Feminism" is the sole scholarly work focusing on *Mother Earth*.

14 Bill Lynskey, "'I Shall Speak in Philadelphia': Emma Goldman and the Free Speech League," *Pennsylvania Magazine of History & Biography* 133, 2 (2009): 167–202; Rebecca Parker, "An Analysis of Emma Goldman's Free Speech Campaign Strategies" (master's thesis, Western Illinois University, 1971).

15 Wexler, *Intimate Life*, 6, 10. For an examination of the lasting effects of Goldman's childhood relationship with her parents, see Alice Wexler, "Early Life of Emma Goldman," *Psychohistory Review* 8, 4 (1980): 7–21.
16 Goldman, *Living My Life*, 11.
17 Wexler, *Intimate Life*, 15–16, 23, 73.
18 Ibid., 21–23, 27; Goldman, *Living My Life*, 11–12.
19 Goldman, *Living My Life*, 11.
20 Ibid., 10.
21 Wexler, *Intimate Life*, 4–6, 23.
22 Goldman, *Living My Life*, 16.
23 John Whiteclay Chambers II, *The Tyranny of Change: America in the Progressive Era, 1900–1917* (New York: St. Martin's Press, 1980), 75; Robert L. Fleegler, *Ellis Island Nation: Immigration Policy and American Identity in the Twentieth Century* (Philadelphia: University of Pennsylvania Press, 2013), 4; Matthew Frye Jacobson, *Barbarian Virtues: The United States Encounters Foreign Peoples at Home and Abroad, 1876–1917* (New York: Hill and Wang, 2000), 6, 61; Wenzer, *Anarchists Adrift*, 30–32.
24 Jacobson, *Barbarian Virtues*, 61–62.
25 Gary Gerstle, *American Crucible: Race and Nation in the Twentieth Century* (Princeton, NJ: Princeton University Press, 2001), 4.
26 Chambers, *Tyranny of Change*, 76; Fleegler, *Ellis Island Nation*, 9–11, 17; Christina A. Ziegler-McPherson, *Americanization in the States: Immigrant Social Welfare Policy, Citizenship, & National Identity in the United States, 1908–1929* (Gainesville: University Press of Florida, 2009), 11.
27 Fleegler, *Ellis Island Nation*, 4; Wenzer, *Anarchists Adrift*, 32.
28 Fleegler, *Ellis Island Nation*, 7; Jacobson, *Barbarian Virtues*, 197.
29 Fleegler, *Ellis Island Nation*, 5.
30 Thomas Mackaman, *New Immigrants and the Radicalization of American Labor, 1914–1924* (Jefferson, NC: McFarland, 2017), 24. Although new immigrants suffered most from turn-of-the-century nativism, some historians note that Jews and Catholics often were perceived as foreign regardless of where they were born or how long they had lived in the U.S. See Fleegler, *Ellis Island Nation*, 5, and Ziegler-McPherson, *Americanization in the States*, 11.
31 Gerstle, *American Crucible*, 4–5, 7; Jacobson, *Barbarian Virtues*, 69; Ziegler-McPherson, *Americanization in the States*, 10.
32 Ziegler-McPherson, *Americanization in the States*, 15.
33 Fleegler, *Ellis Island Nation*, 6.
34 Gerstle, *American Crucible*, 17–18, 50, 59.
35 Jacobson, *Barbarian Virtues*, 4–5, 96.
36 Ibid., 65.
37 Steven L. Piott, *Daily Life in the Progressive Era* (Santa Barbara, CA: Greenwood, 2011), 48.
38 Ibid.; Jacobson, *Barbarian Virtues*, 65; Mackaman, *New Immigrants*, 27, 32–33, 49–51.
39 Goldstene, *Struggle for America's Promise*, 13; Mackaman, *New Immigrants*, 36–37; Michael McGerr, *A Fierce Discontent: The Rise and Fall of the Progressive Movement in America, 1870–1920* (New York: Free Press, 2003), 16–19; Piott, *Daily Life in the Progressive Era*, 65–66.

40 Gerstle, *American Crucible*, 57–58; Jacobson, *Barbarian Virtues*, 180.
41 Piott, *Daily Life in the Progressive Era*, 59, 63. In New York City, 97 percent of clothing manufacturing employees were immigrants or children of immigrants; see Jacobson, *Barbarian Virtues*, 68.
42 Fleegler, *Ellis Island Nation*, 6. For more on the AFL's anti-immigrant views, see Chambers, *Tyranny of Change*, 64, and Mackaman, *New Immigrants*, 52, 69.
43 Piott, *Daily Life in the Progressive Era*, 50–52, 68–69.
44 Chambers, *Tyranny of Change*, 11, 75.
45 Jacobson, *Barbarian Virtues*, 73. See also Gerstle, *American Crucible*, 7.
46 Fleegler, *Ellis Island Nation*, 6.
47 Gornick, *Revolution as a Way of Life*, 18–21. See also Goldstene, *Struggle for America's Promise*, 11, 70; Mackaman, *New Immigrants*, 61; Wenzer, *Anarchists Adrift*, 31–32.
48 Jacobson, *Barbarian Virtues*, 22.
49 Mackaman, *New Immigrants*, 52–58.
50 Goldstene, *Struggle for America's Promise*, 10–11. See also Piott, *Daily Life in the Progressive Era*, 78.
51 Gerstle, *American Crucible*, 100; Jacobson, *Barbarian Virtues*, 89–90.
52 Jacobson, *Barbarian Virtues*, 89.
53 Mackaman, *New Immigrants*, 8.
54 Chambers, *Tyranny of Change*, 65–66; Mackaman, *New Immigrants*, 61–63.
55 Gornick, *Revolution as a Way of Life*, 19.
56 Mackaman, *New Immigrants*, 64–65.
57 Gornick, *Revolution as a Way of Life*, 20.
58 Ibid., 21–22; Goldstene, *Struggle for America's Promise*, 70–72.
59 Gerstle, *American Crucible*, 8.
60 Jacobson, *Barbarian Virtues*, 93.
61 Act of May 6, 1882, ch. 126, 22 *Stat* 58. The Chinese Exclusion Act stayed in place until the 1940s, extended by the Geary Act of 1902 and bolstered by additional anti-Asian legislation passed in 1917 and 1924. Fleegler, *Ellis Island Nation*, 4; Gerstle, *American Crucible*, 23, 60; Bill Ong Hing, *Defining America Through Immigration Policy* (Philadelphia: Temple University Press, 2004), 28–50; Jacobson, *Barbarian Virtues*, 81.
62 Fleegler, *Ellis Island Nation*, 7; Gerstle, *American Crucible*, 53–55.
63 Gerstle, *American Crucible*, 55.
64 Theodore Roosevelt, "First Annual Message," December 3, 1901, at Gerhard Peters and John T. Woolley, *The American Presidency Project*, www.presidency.ucsb.edu/ws/?pid=29542.
65 Act of March 3, 1903, ch. 1012, 32 *Stat* 1222. See also Mary S. Barton, "The Global War on Anarchism: The United States and International Anarchist Terrorism, 1898–1904," *Diplomatic History* 39, 2 (April 2015): 303–330; Alexander Noonan, "'What Must Be the Answer of the United States to Such a Proposition?': Anarchist Exclusion and National Security in the United States, 1887–1903," *Journal of American Studies* 50, 2 (May 2016): 347–76.
66 Thirty-eight immigrants were barred from entering the United States under the 1903 law; fourteen were deported. Jacobson, *Barbarian Virtues*, 95.
67 Act of February 20, 1907, ch. 1184, 34 *Stat* 898.

68 See Oscar S. Straus to Robert Watchorn, November 14, 1907 and November 19, 1907; Bureau of Immigration Memo to Department of Commerce and Labor, November 17, 1907; Oscar S. Straus to Edwin Sims (telegram), March 4, 1908. All of the above in Goldman Papers, reel 56.
69 Reports of the Immigration Commission (Washington: Government Printing Office, 1911). See also Katherine Benton-Cohen, *Inventing the Immigration Problem: The Dillingham Commission and Its Legacy* (Cambridge, MA: Harvard University Press, 2018); Chambers, *Tyranny of Change*, 77; Gerstle, *American Crucible*, 55.
70 Chambers, *Tyranny of Change*, 4, 7; Gerstle, *American Crucible*, 14, 66; Goldstene, *Struggle for America's Promise*, xiv, 15; Jacobson, *Barbarian Virtues*, 18; Piott, *Daily Life in the Progressive Era*, 58, 134–136.
71 Aileen Gallagher, *The Muckrakers: American Journalism during the Age of Reform* (New York: Rosen Publishing, 2006); C. C. Regier, *The Era of the Muckrakers* (Gloucester, MA: Peter Smith, 1957).
72 Goldman, *Living My Life*, 485, 618.
73 Gerstle, *American Crucible*, 7.
74 McGerr, *Fierce Discontent*, 13, 42; Piott, *Daily Life in the Progressive Era*, xiii.
75 Ziegler-McPherson, *Americanization in the States,* 6–10.
76 Gerstle, *American Crucible,* 67.
77 McGerr, *Fierce Discontent*, xiv–xv. See also Ziegler-McPherson, *Americanization in the States*, 11, and Piott, *Daily Life in the Progressive Era*, 155.
78 Mackaman, *New Immigrants*, 24.
79 Ziegler-McPherson, *Americanization in the States*, 9.
80 Ibid., 11.
81 Ibid., 17.
82 McGerr, *Fierce Discontent*, xv; Gerstle, *American Crucible*, 69, 71.
83 Gerstle, *American Crucible*, 71–72, 79.
84 Michael Kazin, *War Against War: The American Fight for Peace, 1914–1918* (New York: Simon & Schuster, 2017), 22–23, 32, 61.
85 John Whiteclay Chambers II, *To Raise An Army: The Draft Comes to Modern America* (New York: Free Press, 1987), 73–124; Kazin, *War Against War*, 23–38; Michael A. Martorelli, "Mobilizing U.S. Industry for the Great War," *Financial History* 123 (Fall 2017): 16–19.
86 Chambers, *To Raise An Army*, 107–115; Kazin, *War Against War*, xi, 20, 38–46.
87 Chambers, *To Raise An Army*, 109; Kazin, *War Against War*, xv. For discussions of the prominent preparedness societies, see John Carver Edwards, "Playing the Patriot Game: The Story of the American Defense Society, 1915–1932," *Studies in History & Society* 1, 1 (1976): 54–72, and Robert D. Ward, "The Origin and Activities of the National Security League, 1914–1919," *Mississippi Valley Historical Review* 47, 1 (January 1960): 51–65.
88 Chambers, *To Raise An Army*, 79–80, 104; Kazin, *War Against War*, 59–65; Jason C. Flanagan, "Woodrow Wilson's 'Rhetorical Restructuring': The

Transformation of the American Self and the Construction of the German Enemy," *Rhetoric & Public Affairs* 7, 2 (2004): 115–148.

89 Kazin, *War Against War*, 82.

90 Act of June 3, 1916, ch. 134, 39 *Stat* 166; Chambers, *To Raise An Army*, 103, 113–115; Flanagan, "Woodrow Wilson's 'Rhetorical Restructuring,'" 121–122; Kazin, *War Against War*, 117.

91 E. Neal Claussen, "'He Kept Us Out of War': Martin H. Glynn's Keynote," *Quarterly Journal of Speech* 51, 1 (1966): 23–32; Chambers, *To Raise An Army*, 121; Kazin, *War Against War*, 114, 124; Y. D. Prasad, "The German-Americans and the Election of 1916," *Indian Journal of American Studies* 11, 1 (1981): 49–57.

92 Chambers, *To Raise An Army*, 127, 132–33; Kazin, *War Against War*, 137, 141–144, 162–163, 177; Sterling Kernek, "The British Government's Reactions to President Wilson's 'Peace' Note of December 1916," *Historical Journal* 13, 4 (1970): 721–766; Robert W. Tucker, "A Benediction on the Past: Woodrow Wilson's War Address," *World Policy Journal* 17, 2 (Summer 2000): 77–93.

93 Flanagan, "Woodrow Wilson's 'Rhetorical Restructuring'"; Joseph M. Siracusa, "American Policy-Makers, World War I, and the Menace of Prussianism, 1914–1920," *Australasian Journal of American Studies* 17, 2 (1998): 1–30.

94 Kazin, *War Against War*, 151–155.

95 For a thorough analysis of conscription in the U.S. before World War I, see Chambers, *To Raise An Army*. For discussions of riots and resistance to the Civil War drafts, see Winona L. Fletcher, "Speechmaking of the New York Draft Riots of 1863," *Quarterly Journal of Speech* 54, 2 (1968): 134–139; William F. Hanna, "The Boston Draft Riot," *Civil War History* 36, 3 (1990): 262–273; Lawrence H. Larsen, "Draft Riot in Wisconsin, 1862," *Civil War History* 7, 4 (1961): 421–427; Peter Levine, "Draft Evasion in the North During the Civil War, 1863–1865," *Journal of American History* 67, 4 (1981): 816–834; Arnold Shankman, "Draft Resistance in Civil War Pennsylvania," *Pennsylvania Magazine of History & Biography* 101, 2 (1977): 190–204; Robert E. Sterling, "Civil War Draft Resistance in Illinois," *Journal of the Illinois State Historical Society* 64, 3 (1971): 244–266.

96 Chambers, *To Raise An Army*, 11.

97 Ibid., 1, 97–98.

98 Kazin, *War Against War*, 111.

99 Chambers, *To Raise An Army*, 119.

100 Act of May 16, 1917, ch. 15, 40 *Stat* 76. For discussion of the conscription debates in Congress, the public, and the press, see Chambers, *To Raise An Army*, 153–176.

101 Kazin, *War Against War*, 203.

102 Chambers, *To Raise An Army*, 205–206. Several scholars have closely examined draft protests as well as racial and ethnic considerations. See, for example, Candice Bredbenner, "A Duty to Defend? The Evolution of Aliens' Military Obligations to the United States, 1792–1946," *Journal*

of Policy History 24, 2 (2012): 224–261; Jeanette Keith, *Rich Man's War, Poor Man's Fight: Race, Class, and Power in the Rural South during the First World War* (Chapel Hill: University of North Carolina Press, 2004); Bill Lynskey, "Reinventing the First Amendment in Wartime Philadelphia," *Pennsylvania Magazine of History & Biography* 131, 1 (2007): 33–80; James Mennell, "African-Americans and the Selective Service Act of 1917," *Journal of Negro History* 84, 3 (1999): 275–287; Erik M. Zissu, "Conscription, Sovereignty, and Land: American Indian Resistance during World War I," *Pacific Historical Review* 64, 4 (1995): 537–566.

103 Michael W. Casey, "The Closing of Cordell Christian College: A Microcosm of American Intolerance During World War I," *Chronicles of Oklahoma* 76, 1 (1998): 20–37; Gerlof D. Homan, "Mennonites and Military Justice in World War I," *Mennonite Quarterly Review* 66, 3 (1992): 365–375; Theodore Kornweibel Jr., "Bishop C. H. Mason and the Church of God in Christ During World War I: The Perils of Conscientious Objection," *Southern Studies: An Interdisciplinary Journal of the South* 26 (Winter 1987): 261–281; Piott, *Daily Life in the Progressive Era,* 226; Sarah D. Shields, "The Treatment of Conscientious Objectors During World War I: Mennonites at Camp Funston," *Kansas History* 4, 4 (1981): 255–269.

104 Chambers, *To Raise An Army*, 206; Robert C. Cottrell, "Roger Nash Baldwin, the National Civil Liberties Bureau, and Intelligence During World War I," *Historian* 60, 1 (Fall 1997): 87–106; Emily Zackin, "The Early ACLU and the Decision to Litigate," *Princeton University Library Chronicle* 67, 3 (Summer 2006): 526–551.

105 *Selective Draft Law Cases*, 245 U.S. 366 (1918); Kazin, *War Against War*, 205.

106 Gerstle, *American Crucible*, 99.

107 Mackaman, *New Immigrants*, 61.

108 Gerstle, *American Crucible*, 97–98; Richard J. Ilkka, "Rhetorical Dramatization in the Development of American Communism," *Quarterly Journal of Speech* 63 (December 1977): 413–427.

109 Gerstle, *American Crucible*, 88–89; Ziegler-McPherson, *Americanization in the States,* 85–88.

110 Ziegler-McPherson, *Americanization in the States*, 88–89.

111 Chambers, *To Raise An Army*, 209; Mackaman, *New Immigrants*, 9.

112 Ziegler-McPherson, *Americanization in the States*, 100. See also Fleegler, *Ellis Island Nation*, 18, and Piott, *Daily Life in the Progressive Era*, 240–241.

113 Gerstle, *American Crucible*, 81–82.

114 Ibid., 92.

115 Mackaman, *New Immigrants*, 87–88; McKerr, *Fierce Discontent*, xvi; Piott, *Daily Life in the Progressive Era,* 240; Ziegler-McPherson, *Americanization in the States*, 84–101.

116 Chambers, *To Raise An Army*, 207; Kazin, *War Against War*, 208; Ziegler-McPherson, *Americanization in the States*, 91–93.

117 Michael Cohen, "'The Ku Klux Government': Vigilantism, Lynching, and the Repression of the IWW," *Journal of the Study of Radicalism* 1, 1 (2007): 31–56; William H. Thomas Jr., *Unsafe for Democracy: World War I and the U.S. Justice Department's Covert Campaign to Suppress Dissent* (Madison: University of Wisconsin Press, 2008), 6.

118 Christopher Capozzola, "The Only Badge Needed Is Your Patriotic Fervor: Vigilance, Coercion, and the Law in World War I America," *Journal of American History* 88, 4 (March 2002): 1364–1367.

119 Ibid.; Cohen, "Ku Klux Government"; Gerstle, *American Crucible*, 93; Philip Jenkins, "'Spy Mad'? Investigating Subversion in Pennsylvania, 1917–1918," *Pennsylvania History* 63, 2 (Spring 1996): 204–231; Mackaman, *New Immigrants*, 9, 98, 107.

120 Kazin, *War Against War*, 209–210; Piott, *Daily Life in the Progressive Era*, 227, 238; Thomas, *Unsafe for Democracy*, 4–6. Goldman detailed Reitman's ordeal in *Living My Life*, 494–503. The June 1912 *Mother Earth* was also dedicated to discussion of the incident and its causes.

121 Thomas, *Unsafe for Democracy*, 4.

122 Chambers, *To Raise An Army*, 211–212.

123 Gerstle, *American Crucible*, 91. See also Fleegler, *Ellis Island Nation*, 11.

124 Christopher Capozzola, "Legacies for Citizenship: Pinpointing Americans during and after World War I," *Diplomatic History* 38, 4 (2014), 716; Kimberly Jensen, "From Citizens to Enemy Aliens: Oregon Women, Marriage, and the Surveillance State during the First World War," *Oregon Historical Quarterly* 114, 4 (Winter 2013): 453–473.

125 Woodrow Wilson, "Third Annual Message," December 7, 1915, at Peters and Woolley, *The American Presidency Project*, www.presidency.ucsb.edu/ws/index.php?pid=29556. Congress did not pass the two laws until after the United States declared war, more than a year after the speech.

126 The act also expanded restriction of Asian immigration and barred entry for homosexual immigrants. Act of February 5, 1917, ch. 29, 39 *Stat* 874; Capozzola, "Legacies for Citizenship," 718–719; Gerstle, *American Crucible*, 96; Hing, *Defining America*, 51–61.

127 Act of October 16, 1918, ch. 186, 40 *Stat* 1012; Capozzola, "Legacies for Citizenship," 719; Gerstle, *American Crucible*, 99.

128 Gerstle, *American Crucible*, 95. See also Robert K. Murray, *Red Scare: A Study in National Hysteria, 1919–1920* (Minneapolis: University of Minnesota Press, 1955), 211.

129 Fleegler, *Ellis Island Nation*, 12; McGerr, *Fierce Discontent*, xvi; Murray, *Red Scare*.

130 Gerstle, *American Crucible*, 99; Mackaman, *New Immigrants*, 5, 88–89; Murray, *Red Scare*, 7–17; Piott, *Daily Life in the Progressive Era*, 250.

131 See Nunzio Pernicone, "Galleani and Italian Anarchist Terrorism in the United States," *Studi Emigrazione* (Italian) 30, 111 (1993): 469–489; Jeffrey Simon, "The Forgotten Terrorists: Lessons from the History of Terrorism," *Terrorism and Political Violence* 20, 2 (Summer 2008): 195–214.

132 Beverly Gage, *The Day Wall Street Exploded: A Story of America in Its First Age of Terror* (Oxford: Oxford University Press, 2009), 208. Some

of Goldman's contributions to *Cronaca Sovversiva* are collected in the Goldman Papers, reels 47, 48, and 49.

133 Gage, *The Day Wall Street Exploded*, 209–210.

134 Presumably the senders intended the bombs to be delivered on May 1, which historically had been an international labor holiday. Hardwick's maid lost her hands in the blast. Gage, *The Day Wall Street Exploded*, 211; Murray, *Red Scare*, 69–73.

135 Gage, *The Day Wall Street Exploded*, 119, 211; Murray, *Red Scare*, 78–79.

136 Gage, *The Day Wall Street Exploded*, 211.

137 Ibid., 120–122, 128–129; Murray, *Red Scare*, 80–8, 196–197, 207; Piott, *Daily Life in the Progressive Era*, 256.

2 Uncertain Times for Freedom of Expression

Standing in a federal courtroom on a summer day in 1917, Emma Goldman delivered closing arguments in her trial for conspiring to obstruct the military draft. She warned the jury that democracy suffers when free speech and a free press are restricted by onerous government laws and crackdowns on unpopular ideas. Furthermore, she asked how the world could take America seriously "when democracy at home is daily being outraged, free speech suppressed, peaceable assemblies broken up by overbearing and brutal gangsters in uniform; when free press is curtailed and every independent opinion gagged." She wondered, "Verily, poor as we are in democracy, how can we give of it to the world?"[1] The assumptions behind her free expression-based argument in the New York courtroom that day directly conflicted with Judge Julius Mayer's instructions to the jury on the first day of the trial. He explained to the jurors that the case had nothing to do with freedom of expression, contending that although free speech was guaranteed under the Constitution, "free speech means not license, not counseling disobedience of the law. Free speech means that frank, full and orderly expression which every man and woman in this land, citizen or alien engages in."[2] In short, Judge Mayer told the jury not to consider freedom of expression concerns because the case at hand did not qualify for such protections.

These largely opposing conceptualizations of the meanings and boundaries of First Amendment safeguards for free expression—placed in stark contrast within the same courtroom at the start and end of Goldman's trial—in many ways represented the uncertainty that surrounded such rights during this period. Goldman's trial and conviction in federal court, along with her fight to avoid deportation in the final days of 1919, can be understood as a final chapter to an extended period of uncertainty about the meaning of free expression in the United States—a period one respected historian labeled the "forgotten years" for free speech. The era was influenced from its outset by the Constitutional limitations placed on the powers of the federal government by a Supreme Court that had not yet come to grips with its tenuous place as an unelected, largely unaccountable body with the power to strike down laws that democratically elected lawmakers voted on and presidents signed.[3] This period in the Court's development included a slow change in how freedom of expression was understood. The change occurred alongside a variety of battles that involved civil rights and social change.

Prior to the Civil War, Constitutional safeguards, such as those found in the First Amendment, did not extend to state-based matters, thus leaving each state to create its own limitations on expression.[4] After the Civil War, the Fourteenth Amendment required equal protection under the law for all United States citizens, thus creating a bridge by which federal protections extended to the states.[5] Problematically, despite the amendment's ratification in 1868, the Supreme Court largely rejected its promise. In its first major brush with the new amendment five years after its ratification, justices, by a five-to-four vote, concluded that states retain exclusive powers to regulate human rights. The Court reasoned:

> Under the pressure of all the excited feeling growing out of the war, our statesmen have still believed that the existence of the States with powers for domestic and local government, including the regulation of civil rights – the rights of person and of property – was essential to the perfect working of our complex form of government.[6]

As a result of this precedent and others like it from the post-Civil War period, the Court took several decades to gradually uphold Constitutionally promised rights in state-related cases. Justices first extended freedom of expression rights to state matters in *Gitlow v. New York* in 1925. This step forward, however, did not mark a substantial change in how justices treated unpopular ideas. While anarchist Benjamin Gitlow's case remains a crucial decision because it set the precedent that First Amendment guarantees supersede all laws, not just federal ones, he still lost his case. A majority of the Supreme Court did not support a decision on the basis of freedom of expression until *Near v. Minnesota* in 1931.[7]

Importantly, Goldman's years in the United States—from when she stepped off a steamer in New York in 1885 until she was rather unceremoniously placed on an Army ship on a winter day in 1919—coincided with the final portion of this uncertain period regarding civil liberties. During these years, the nation struggled with civil rights, particularly regarding freedom of expression. Mounting pressures regarding workers' rights, women's rights, and, ultimately, the passage of the Selective Service Act in May 1917 and the Espionage Act a month later, pushed the courts and legal scholars to more carefully consider the meaning of free expression. As political scientist Mark Graber explained, "The political status of expression rights slowly changed over the first fifteen years of the twentieth century."[8] With her essays in *Mother Earth* and her speaking engagements around the country, as well as with her trial as the United States's involvement in World War I continued to grow, Goldman contributed to this broader awakening to freedom of expression concerns and the increasing pressure the courts experienced to clarify the meanings of First Amendment safeguards.

This chapter contextualizes the legal and freedom-of-expression environment that surrounded and influenced Goldman's work—before, during, and after her trial and conviction in 1917. The chapter considers how the Supreme Court conceptualized expression and other rights during the years leading up to Goldman's trial before examining a group of crucial post-World War I cases that occurred between her 1917 conviction and 1919 deportation.

Judicial Reasoning in the *Lochner* Era

During Goldman's years in the United States, she and other radicals faced a judicial system that was "hostile to virtually all free speech claims."[9] The roots of such hostilities were not exclusive to free expression-related cases. They were part of the broader development of how the Supreme Court understood its role during the final decades of the nineteenth century and into the twentieth. The Court, as an institution, entered the Civil War era in disarray. The *Dred Scott v. Sandford* decision in 1857—in which justices concluded that Dred Scott, a former slave who sued for his freedom, was not a citizen and therefore did not have rights—was met with significant backlash.[10] President Abraham Lincoln derided the Court's conclusion as "erroneous," picking it apart in a speech later that year.[11] Charles Evans Hughes, who served on the Court from 1910 to 1916 and again as chief justice from 1930–1941, labeled the ruling as one of the few instances when the Court "suffered severely from self-inflicted wounds."[12] After the Civil War started, Chief Justice Roger Taney, who authored the *Dred Scott* decision, concluded that Lincoln could not suspend the Constitutional rights of a Maryland secessionist held in a military prison. The Court asserted that John Merryman had a right to be charged and tried in a court of his peers. Chief Justice Taney ordered that Merryman be brought before him. The president refused to follow the chief justice's order, and Merryman remained in military custody.[13]

By the time the Court reached the *Lochner* era, which emerged late in the Reconstruction period and persisted until the Great Depression, it had recovered its confidence and perhaps added to it substantially. The *Lochner* era earned its name from one of the Court's most infamous decisions from the period and is the judicial regime that characterized Goldman's life and work in the United States. During this period, justices regularly and assuredly reviewed and overturned Congressional actions and presidential initiatives.[14] Essentially, the Court had gone from the subordinate, "least dangerous" branch of government before the Civil War to an empowered body that felt it played a crucial role in protecting what it believed were the country's best interests.[15] Supreme Court historian Robert McCloskey likened the Court's attitude during the period to that of a "medieval knight-bachelor" who had served his time as a squire and was now a newly minted defender, ready to "slay all the dragons."[16] Among the "dragons" was socialism. Justices generally believed that the Supreme Court had a duty to protect free enterprise from social interventions and social change in general, even when officials elected by democratic majorities authored, passed, and signed such laws.[17] Such an understanding by justices aligned substantially with Social Darwinism, which Herbert Spencer popularized in the middle of the nineteenth century; the "survival of the fittest" mentality supported laissez-faire capitalism and opposed reform.[18]

Though he ascribed to some of Spencer's beliefs, Justice Oliver Wendell Holmes's dissent in *Lochner v. New York* (1905) accused the Court's majority of inappropriately incorporating Spencer's ideas into its decision-making.[19] *Lochner* involved a New York law that limited bakery employees to a sixty-hour workweek. The law was passed with the health and safety of the workers in mind, but the Court found the law unconstitutional because justices understood it as infringing upon the business owner's liberty. They reasoned, "The freedom of master and employe [*sic*] to contract with each other in relation to their employment, and in defining the same, cannot be prohibited or interfered with, without violating the Federal Constitution."[20] Justice Holmes, in a brief but long-remembered dissent, contended that the Court's majority should have set its economic theories aside and deferred to the people's will in this case. He explained, "I strongly believe that my agreement or disagreement has nothing to do with the right of a majority to embody their opinions into law."[21] The decision, which was announced less than a year before Goldman published the first issue of *Mother Earth*, has persisted as one of the most recognized examples of judicial intrusion into the political realm in the Court's history.[22] It is, crucially for our purposes, illustrative of the Court's attitude during Goldman's years in the United States.

Importantly, *Lochner* was not a judicial aberration. The Court constructed similar reasoning in a child-labor case less than a year before Goldman's arrest in 1917. In *Hammer v. Dagenhart*, the Court struck down the Keating-Owen Child Labor Act, which criminalized the interstate shipment of products produced by child labor. By making the

Figure 2.1 Justice Oliver Wendell Holmes was central to developing how the Supreme Court viewed freedom of expression.

Source: Library of Congress.

matter an interstate commerce concern, Congress had sought to work around relatively recent precedents such as the *Slaughterhouse Cases*, which generally concluded that the Constitution did not allow the government to regulate the activities of the states.[23] After all, the Court specifically had stated in the 1895 antitrust case *United States v. E.C.*

Knight that the federal government could not regulate manufacturing but could regulate interstate commerce.[24] Despite the *E.C. Knight* precedent, justices struck down Congress's child-labor law in *Hammer* by a five-to-four vote. The Court concluded that "the powers not expressly delegated to the National Government are reserved" to the states.[25] Thus, in the absence of a clear Constitutional mandate, the Court reasoned that if something is not covered in the Constitution, it cannot be regulated by the federal government. As McCloskey contended, the decision was based on "limitations previously unknown," rather than precedent or Constitutional guidance.[26] The Court used similar logic to strike down another Congressional attempt to limit child labor in 1922. While writing the Revenue Act of 1919, Congress included a 10-percent tax on the profits of any company that employed child laborers. While the Court recognized that Congress had the Constitutional authority to levy taxes, justices struck down the provision because they viewed it not as a tax but as a penalty. Chief Justice Howard Taft, writing for the Court, explained that the provision was "solely to the achievement of some other purpose plainly within state power."[27] The Court found the provision to be unconstitutional because Congress's *intent* was to limit child labor, rather than to raise revenue for the government.

Thus, in these instances along with others during this period, the Court—often with limited Constitutional support—overturned laws passed and signed by officials that democratic majorities had elected. Furthermore, seven years after *Hammer* and four years after Goldman's deportation, the Court struck down a minimum-wage law using similar reasoning.[28] It was not until the "switch in time that saved nine" in 1937 that the Court started yielding to mounting popular and political pressures it faced to set its political and social agendas aside when the law in question did not raise a clear constitutional question. The switch corresponded with a threat from President Franklin Roosevelt that he would "pack" the Supreme Court with enough justices to get New Deal legislation past the Court if justices did not reevaluate their approach to the law.[29]

From Silencing Dissent to Conceptualizing a Marketplace of Ideas

As the Court dispatched a variety of Congressional efforts to improve conditions for workers, slay the "dragon" of socialism, and safeguard free enterprise, it began to face challenges on a relatively new front. The Espionage Act of 1917 and the Sedition Act of 1918 led to a wave of arrests and challenges. These acts officially codified and criminalized broad swaths of expression that, in preceding decades, were either tolerated or inconsistently prosecuted using a patchwork of state and local laws and jurisdictionally applied legal interpretations. Importantly, these massively encompassing federal acts were largely aimed at ideas communicated by the very socialists whose economic policies the Supreme Court had been carefully guarding the nation from for decades. Ultimately, with the World War I acts, the Court suddenly faced a new wave of free expression questions that generally had remained outside of its concern. Legal scholar David Rabban concluded that these two acts helped lead to a "shared reaction against the repression of speech during and after World War I."[30]

The Espionage Act, signed into law on the same day that Goldman and Berkman were arrested, made it a crime for any person to communicate in a way that interfered with military operations, supported enemy activities, encouraged disloyalty among military personnel, or obstructed the draft.[31] According to historian Margaret Blanchard, President Woodrow Wilson believed he needed to stifle criticism and silence voices of discontent if he were to lead a united force into war.[32] The law was used to prosecute about 2,000 speakers and writers.[33] It also hampered published expression via a controversial provision that empowered Postmaster General Albert Burleson to exclude from the mails—without court approval—any matter he interpreted as willful obstruction to the war's progress. He particularly targeted anti-conscription materials. Though legal scholars disagree, contemporary liberals deemed this a carte-blanche power of censorship. Its execution effectively suppressed more than 100 periodicals—including Goldman's *Mother Earth*—as well as numerous pamphlets and books.[34] In 1918, Congress added the Sedition Act, which further limited anti-war speech by criminalizing the use of "disloyal, profane, scurrilous, or abusive language intended to cause contempt or scorn for the United States, the Constitution, or the flag."[35]

Patterson v. Colorado, in 1907, served as an ideological pre-cursor to the flurry of Espionage cases in 1918 and 1919. World War I-era laws' widespread prohibition of expression, and government agents' enthusiastic use of them, ultimately led the Court to do something it never had done before—squarely interpret the First Amendment. Before that period, however, *Patterson* marked the closest the Court came to addressing the First Amendment's promises. Coming two years after *Lochner*, the 1907 case involved a contempt charge against Sen. Thomas Patterson, whose Denver newspaper printed cartoons and opinion pieces questioning the motives of Colorado Supreme Court justices.[36] The Colorado court contended that the cartoons commented on pending cases and were intended to "embarrass the court in the impartial administration of justice."[37] Patterson argued that the case the cartoons addressed had been decided and no appeal had been filed. The Senator further argued that he had a right under both the state and federal constitutions to communicate truthful information. The Court was not sympathetic to his claims. In one of the first references to freedom of speech in the Court's history, Justice Holmes drew from a centuries-old interpretation of free expression law to explain that

> the main purpose of such constitutional provisions is "to prevent all such *previous restraints* upon publications as had been practiced by other governments," and they do not prevent the subsequent punishment of such as may be deemed contrary to the public welfare.[38]

In constructing his reasoning, Justice Holmes cited *Respublica v. Oswald*, a 1788 case that predates the First Amendment, and *Commonwealth v. Blanding*, an 1825 free press case from his home state of Massachusetts. Aside from the noticeable absence of First Amendment precedent from which the jurist could draw, the most noteworthy feature of his citations is that they both dealt with instances when judges drew a line between protected and unprotected speech. That line, as Rabban highlighted, emanated from British common law and limited freedom of expression protections to prior government restraints. In other words, it allowed for individuals to be penalized *after* communicating their ideas but not before.[39] Judge Mayer demonstrated a similar understanding of free expression when he instructed the jury not to consider First Amendment claims during Goldman's trial.

While Justice Holmes dispatched Sen. Patterson's First Amendment claims in the Court's opinion without ever actually naming the amendment, Justice John Marshall Harlan dissented. The two justices, both decorated Civil War veterans, often took opposing sides. In fact, Supreme Court historian Jeffrey Rosen characterized the two jurists' personalities as opposed in almost every way. Rosen described Justice Holmes as "elegant, bloodless, aristocratic, and aloof," whereas Justice Harlan was "emotional, gregarious, and prone to delivering extemporaneous stump speeches in open court."[40] When it came to *Patterson*, Justice Harlan delivered a stinging counter to Justice Holmes's opinion for the Court. Though Justice Holmes is remembered as perhaps the nation's greatest legal mind and a First Amendment hero, it was Justice Harlan's understandings in the *Patterson* dissent that emerged half a century later as the dominant view of the First Amendment's meaning.[41] He contended that free speech and a free press,

> belonging to every citizen of the United States, constitute essential parts of every man's liberty, and are protected against violation by that clause of the Fourteenth Amendment forbidding a State to deprive any person of his liberty without due process of law.[42]

Although Justice Harlan represented the strongest voice for freedom of expression rights in his *Patterson* dissent, he died in 1911, well before Goldman's appeal and the landmark cases of 1919 reached the Court. Importantly, however, in this period, his understandings were gravely outside of the Court's judicial philosophy. Justice Harlan's dissent both framed freedom of expression in broader terms and incorporated it to the states via the Fourteenth Amendment, a step a majority of the Court would not take for another eighteen years.

As Rabban noted in *Free Speech in the Forgotten Years*, historians and legal scholars traditionally have identified *Schenck v. United States* in 1919 "as the Supreme Court's initial confrontation with the meaning of free speech."[43] Goldman's 1917 Supreme Court appeal as well as *Baltzer v. United States*, an unpublished decision involving an early Espionage Act conviction, suggest that while *Schenck* might have been the most significant brush with free expression questions, it was not the Court's first. Goldman and Emmanuel Baltzer's cases are often overlooked because of their details and timing, which are explained below. Conversely, the facts, timing, and legal reasoning in *Schenck* and *Abrams v. United States* later that year set them apart. Placed in context, however, *Goldman* and *Baltzer* set the stage for the landmark rulings that followed. Indeed, the makeup of the Court did not change between 1916 and 1922. Thus, the same nine justices that rejected Goldman's appeal in January 1918 decided *Abrams* in November 1919. Despite this consistency of *who* was on the Court during this period, the Court's legal philosophy regarding the First Amendment changed significantly.

Before 1919: Goldman and Baltzer

Emmanuel Baltzer was among thirty German-Americans arrested in South Dakota on August 28, 1917, for violating the Espionage Act, signed into law just more than two months earlier. According to the *New York Times*'s front-page, above-the-fold account, the men were brought to federal court and charged with violating the act because they wrote a letter to the state's governor protesting the Selective Service Act.[44] The authors of the letter explained that, if their demands for reform in the Selective Service Act were not met, they would not vote for the governor in the next election. The letter was not made public and did not include any threats to physically impede the draft.[45] On the same day federal officials rounded up the letter-writers in South Dakota, authorities arrested socialist leaders Charles Schenck and Elizabeth Baer in Philadelphia. Schenck and Baer were arrested for violating the Espionage Act after they oversaw the printing and distribution of about 15,000 leaflets to men who had been drafted. The leaflets encouraged the men not to report for service, contending that they should "not submit to intimidation" and instead should petition for the conscription act's repeal.[46] Both arrests came about six weeks after Goldman and Berkman had been convicted in federal court for obstructing the draft. By late December, as the Supreme Court deliberated on *Goldman v. United States*, Schenck and Baer had been convicted in federal court of "conspiracy to undermine the Selective Conscription act," according to the *Philadelphia Inquirer*'s account from the trial.[47]

Both August 1917 Espionage Act arrests were destined for the Supreme Court, but scholars often ignore Goldman's appeal as the first case related to draft obstruction that reached the Court's docket. Legal scholar Sheldon Novick, for example, contended that *Baltzer* was the first draft-related obstruction case to reach the Supreme Court.[48] *Baltzer*, however, did not reach the Court until November 1918, nearly a year after Goldman's appeal was heard and ten months after it was decided. This discrepancy can be attributed at least partially to the nature of the charges Goldman faced. Although she appealed a conviction for obstructing the draft, Goldman, unlike those who followed her, was charged with violating the Selective Service Act rather than the Espionage Act. The Court's short, unanimous decision to uphold her conviction also is distinctive in that it was the final case of its kind in which justices made no mention of the First Amendment.

The justices heard Goldman's appeal on the same two days in December 1917 as the *Selective Draft Law Cases*, a collective name for seven challenges to the constitutionality of the Selective Service Act, which had been signed that spring.[49] Goldman's lawyer and friend Harry Weinberger made several arguments on her behalf, most of which revolved around the Selective Service Act's unconstitutionality and Goldman's belief that she did not violate the law by speaking against the draft. Documents Weinberger filed with the Supreme Court in July and November of 1917 cited the First Amendment, but they only explicitly explored provisions regarding religion—not freedom of expression. As part of Weinberger's assertions of the Selective Service Act's unconstitutionality, he stated that the law privileged members of religious sects whose creeds forbade participation in war. Therefore, Goldman's attorney argued, the law "prohibits and invades the free exercise of the religion" of any individuals who did not belong to those sects.[50] Weinberger also asserted that authorities had not provided evidence of conspiracy. They had not proven that Goldman had counseled anyone against registering; in fact, Weinberger demonstrated Goldman's belief it was not her place to give such advice. Furthermore, Goldman's attorney declared that authorities could not prove any men of draft age had heard or read her words, much less that anyone failed to register because of her words.[51] According to Weinberger, all authorities had demonstrated in Goldman's federal court trial was that she had

Figure 2.2 A news photographer captured this image of Goldman on a streetcar with her attorney Harry Weinberger and her co-defendant Alexander Berkman in 1917, ironically seated under a patriotic advertising placard.

Source: Library of Congress.

expressed opinions about the war and the draft. In the only nod to free expression principles within Weinberger's argument, he insisted,

> The expression of disapproval is necessary before any law can be changed, before Congress can know what the people want, but that does not mean that those who express that disapproval are urging people to break or resist the law.[52]

The Court was unsympathetic, concluding that some of the arguments were "absolutely devoid of merit" and upholding Goldman's conviction. By the time the Court decided Goldman's case, justices had ruled that the Selective Service Act did not violate the Thirteenth Amendment's ban on involuntary servitude because each citizen was obligated to perform "his supreme and noble duty of contributing to the defense of the right and honor of the nation," and the law itself was an expression of the people's will because the war was declared "by the great representative body of the people."[53] The act's constitutionality and laws regarding conspiracy formed the bases of their *Goldman* decision, which was announced a week after the Selective Service Act ruling. The Court argued that Goldman's actions constituted conspiracy and were punishable even if no one carried out the acts she recommended.[54] Therefore, the Court avoided explicitly addressing free expression concerns in Goldman's case.

Baltzer's case was different because he was convicted for obstructing the draft under the Espionage Act, not the Selective Service Act. The Court heard the *Baltzer* appeal in November 1918, a month after Abrams was in a New York federal courtroom with Weinberger at his side. When justices gathered in late November to take an initial vote, they were not unanimous—to the consternation of Chief Justice Edward White. Justice Holmes, who was joined by Justice Louis Brandeis, stated that he planned to dissent; he distributed a draft of his dissent on December 3. The first half of the opinion focused on the facts of the case, with the jurist pointing out that Baltzer and his cohort were very likely ignorant and misguided in their efforts to compel the governor of South Dakota to enact the desired changes to the Selective Service Act and how the war was being funded.[55] Late in the opinion, however, Holmes's tone shifted to broader thoughts about freedom of expression during wartime. He explained, "I think our intention to put out all our powers in aid of success in war should not hurry us into intolerance of opinions and speech that could not be imagined to do harm, although opposed to our own."[56] Importantly, he followed this passage with a reference to the Bill of Rights, emphasizing that it "cost so much blood to establish," that it "still is worth fighting for, and that no tittle of it should be abridged."[57] Legal scholars have been struggling to reconcile this passage with Justice Holmes's opinions from the period since the unpublished *Baltzer* dissent was discovered among his papers in the late 1980s. The jurist left room for limitations to freedom of expression when he allowed that "real obstructions of law, giving real aid and comfort to the enemy, I should have been glad to see punished."[58] The *Baltzer* opinion, however, shows a greater concern for free expression than Justice Holmes demonstrated in his *Patterson* opinion a decade earlier. It also conveys a more encompassing view of how he understood free expression and its value to society than is evident in the three unanimous, Espionage Act-related opinions he later wrote for the Court in spring 1919. In fact, Justice Holmes's reasoning in the unpublished *Baltzer* opinion is far closer in tone to his dissent in *Abrams*, the fall 1919 decision in which he famously brought forth the marketplace of ideas theory of the First Amendment.[59]

Justice Holmes's decision to dissent in *Baltzer* placed Chief Justice White, as the steward of the Court's reputation and place in society, in a difficult position. The chief justice faced pressure from President Wilson and Congress for the Court to deliver a unanimous opinion in its first Espionage Act case, particularly because it was a draft obstruction conviction. Chief Justice White wrote, "please stall" on Justice Holmes's draft dissent.[60] After reading the draft, Justice Brandeis wrote that he agreed with Chief Justice White about waiting to release the ruling. He explained, "I think in decency – this case should be held until the many involving the same and similar positions – advanced for January – are heard."[61] The wait would not be necessary, however. About two weeks after Justice Holmes submitted his draft dissent to the other justices, the Justice Department communicated to the Court that it had made an error and dropped the *Baltzer* case.[62] The nature of the error is not clear, but Justice Holmes's draft dissent—a would-be stepping stone between the Court's reasoning in *Goldman* and its far clearer, First Amendment-oriented ruling in the *Schenck* decision—was lost in the shuffle of Justice Holmes's voluminous correspondences and drafts.

The First Amendment's Day in Court: Schenck, Debs, and Frohwerk

The Court did not have to wait long before facing similar legal questions. As Goldman sewed coats, jackets, and overalls in the Missouri penitentiary, the justices deliberated upon the three Espionage Act cases before them.[63] Justices heard Schenck's appeal on January 9 and 10, 1919, less than a month after the government dropped its case against Baltzer. The socialist leaders had been found guilty of violating the Espionage Act and had a second hearing in the District Court of Eastern Pennsylvania during the fall of 1918. Schenck and Baer's arguments that the government lacked sufficient evidence to convict

Figure 2.3 Socialist leader Eugene V. Debs addresses an Ohio Socialist Party convention in Canton on June 16, 1918; he was arrested for the speech under the Espionage Act.

Source: National Archives.

them did not sway the district judge. He produced a terse five hundred-word decision that upheld their conviction, and the duo appealed to the Supreme Court.[64]

Nearly three weeks after hearing Schenck's case, justices had not yet ruled on it when they heard Eugene Debs's and Jacob Frohwerk's appeals. In June 1918, Debs—whom Goldman admired as a kindred spirit—was arrested for the ideas he communicated during his address to the Ohio Socialist Party convention in Canton earlier that month.[65] During his speech, he asserted that the working men who shed their blood fighting the ruling class's battles never had a voice in declaring war or making peace. Objecting to the war on behalf of the workers, Debs called on laborers to organize "along revolutionary industrial lines" to conquer public power and bring permanent peace to the world.[66] The speech also included commentary on curtailed freedom of expression during the war: "It is extremely dangerous to exercise the constitutional right of free speech in a country fighting to make democracy safe for the world." Debs emphasized that he had to be careful during his remarks because "there are certain limitations placed upon the right of free speech."[67] He was not careful enough. A Cleveland federal court found Debs guilty of violating the Espionage Act in September 1918. Speaking on his own behalf the final day of the trial, Debs cited the First Amendment and asked the audience "isn't it strange that we Socialists stand almost alone in defending the constitution of the United States today?"[68] He continued, in a speech that Goldman later read from her prison cell, "It is far more dangerous to attempt to gag a free people than to permit them to speak."[69] The *Cleveland Plain-Dealer* published substantial portions of his speech in the next day's paper, notching the story underneath a large, bold, seven-column headline about men reporting for the draft that day.

On the same day Supreme Court justices heard Debs's case, they heard arguments regarding Frohwerk, editor of the German-language *Missouri Staats-Zeitung*. Frohwerk's German heritage automatically subjected him to hostility from his American neighbors in the xenophobic war-time atmosphere; his support of the German war cause in newspaper columns and speeches increased the ill will. While Frohwerk argued that German-Americans were loyal to and productive in their new nation, he also criticized the American government for supporting the Allied cause against his home country. Like Goldman and Debs, Frohwerk cited capitalist causes for American and British involvement in the war and lamented that conscription forced men to risk their lives for the nation's rich. Authorities arrested Frohwerk under the Espionage Act on January 26, 1918, for editorials published from June to December 1917. Frohwerk appealed his case to the Supreme Court, arguing that he had been deprived of his constitutional right to be heard in court because the judge at his trial delivered a twenty-five-page opinion denying Frohwerk's motion to dismiss after only a five-minute recess. Furthermore, the jury deliberated for only three minutes. Frohwerk believed the court had decided his guilt before he ever stepped in the courtroom.[70]

By the time the Supreme Court heard *Schenck*, *Debs*, and *Frohwerk*, the war that spurred the Espionage and Sedition laws had been over for more than two months. In March 1919, the Court announced its verdicts for all three cases on the same day. Justices unanimously upheld the convictions under the Espionage Act and, in doing so, found the law to be constitutional. Justice Holmes wrote all three of the decisions, with *Schenck* providing the clearest rationale regarding the Court's reasoning and understanding of the First Amendment. In a relatively short opinion, Justice Holmes returned, briefly, to his reasoning from *Patterson*, explaining that freedom of expression could be seen only as a prohibition against expression before it is communicated, thus leaving the government free to punish ideas after they are shared. He pivoted, however, to a different line of reasoning, which ultimately led to the "clear and present danger" test that would dominate the Court in sedition-related cases for the next half century. Justice Holmes contended that the circumstances of the actions in question were of crucial concern. He explained that "the most stringent protection of free speech would not protect a man in falsely shouting fire in a theatre and causing a panic."[71] The Court, in its unanimity, thus agreed—for the first time in its history—that freedom of expression could be limited and the promise that "Congress shall make no law … abridging the freedom of speech, or of the press" found in the First Amendment does not absolutely ban all limitations on expression.[72] Justice Holmes contextualized his conclusion that Congress should have a right to halt speech that can bring about "substantive evils" by highlighting that what can and cannot be communicated might be different during war versus peace time.[73] Citing Goldman's appeal to the Supreme Court as precedent to uphold Schenck's conviction, Justice Holmes indicated that speech aiming to instigate an act was dangerous regardless of whether the speech was successful.[74]

As unqualified and direct as Justice Holmes's reasoning was in the Court's three unanimous 1919 Espionage Act opinions, he expressed some concern to a friend two weeks later. He lamented the decisions, stating, "I greatly regretted having to write them – and (between ourselves) that the government pressed them to a hearing."[75] He expressed little sympathy for Debs, suggesting he could "split his guts without my interfering," and justified the decisions by explaining that "on the only questions before us I could not doubt about the law."[76] Justice Holmes was not the only one who lamented the rulings. Zechariah Chafee, a friend of Justice Holmes's who was among the leaders of Harvard Law School and one of the leading legal scholars in the nation, published an extensive, constructive critique of the Court's rulings in *Schenck*, *Debs,* and *Frohwerk*. The article, "Freedom of Speech in War Time," persists as one of the landmark statements about how First Amendment protections should be understood. It appeared in *Harvard Law Review* in June, between the Court's spring 1919 Espionage Act rulings and the *Abrams* appeal that awaited the Court when it returned from summer recess. Crucially, the article's timing made it part of the legal and scholarly communities' discovery of the First Amendment in the years that immediately followed Goldman's 1917 appeal. In fact, Chafee included an extended footnote about Goldman's federal court trial, highlighting Judge Mayer's statement to the jury regarding the limitations of free speech.[77]

Chafee rather surgically dissected Justice Holmes's reasoning, concluding that, in short, his friend and the rest of the Court had gotten it wrong. He explained that the Court had "a magnificent opportunity to make articulate for us that major premise, under which judges ought to classify words as inside or outside the scope of the First Amendment."[78]

He contended that Judge Learned Hand's reasoning in an Espionage Act case decided in July 1917, just after Goldman's federal court trial, was more in line with the First Amendment's meaning. In *Masses v. Patten*, New York City's postmaster had refused under the Espionage Act to allow copies of *The Masses*, a socialist magazine, to go through the mail. The *Masses* issue in question included substantial references to Goldman's trial, including a poetic tribute to her plight.[79] At the time of the case, Judge Hand was a respected federal court judge in New York. He graduated from Harvard Law School and looked up to Justice Holmes.[80] Judge Hand reasoned in *Masses* that the postmaster did not have the right to withhold the magazine from distribution simply because it communicated anti-war sentiments. Justice Hand concluded:

> to assimilate agitation, legitimate as such, with direct incitement to violent resistance, is to disregard the tolerance of all methods of political agitation which in normal times is a safeguard of free government. The distinction is not a scholastic subterfuge, but a hard-bought acquisition in the fight for freedom.[81]

Chafee lauded this passage, contending that "there is no finer statement of the right of free speech than these words."[82] Judge Hand did not agree with the Court's rulings in the spring 1919 Espionage Act cases. Just as Chafee's article was being published, Hand ran into Justice Holmes on a train. Having finished their cases for the term, both were on their way to their summer recesses—Justice Holmes to his beloved Beverly Farms in Massachusetts and Judge Hand to New Hampshire. Judge Hand spoke to the elder jurist and made his case for a different approach.[83] This was not a new topic of conversation for the two. The only difference was the new decisions. A year earlier, the two had shared a correspondence about judicial philosophy that touched upon the nature of truth and the value of hard-and-fast judicial approaches.[84] The two also exchanged correspondence about Judge Hand's *Masses* decision. In a February 1919 letter, Justice Holmes stated that he had read the ruling and disagreed with it, though he "thought that few judges indeed would have put their view with such force and such admirable form."[85] The date of the letter indicates Justice Holmes essentially had Judge Hand's alternative, more nuanced approach to freedom of expression on his desk when he was drafting the three Espionage Act opinions between January and March 1919. Furthermore, Judge Hand directly questioned Justice Holmes about the rulings in an April 1919 letter. Justice Holmes was dismissive, as he was on the train two months later, of Judge Hand's questions about what he meant in the rulings. Justice Holmes replied to Judge Hand by stating that he did not understand his point or how their two approaches differed. He explained, "You said the responsibility only began when the words were directly an incitement. I am afraid I don't see how you differ from the test as stated by me in Schenck." Justice Holmes continued with a long quote from his *Schenck* opinion, concluding that, "I don't know what the matter is, or how we differ."[86]

Abrams and the Marketplace of Ideas

Justice Holmes's dissent in *Abrams v. United States* later that year suggests he reflected on Judge Hand's comments, as well as Chafee's critique. Exchanges among Justice Holmes, Judge Hand, and Chafee—three of the most respected legal minds in the nation's history regarding freedom of expression during the summer of 1919—provide crucial information regarding the emerging differences in First Amendment interpretation as the Court heard *Abrams* on October 21 and 22, 1919. Goldman was released from prison in late September but was quickly summoned to appear before an immigration judge on Ellis Island. As her attorney Weinberger prepared for that trial, scheduled for the last week of October, he also had an appearance before the Supreme Court to contend with. Weinberger argued that the federal court lacked sufficient evidence to convict Jacob Abrams and his cohort under the Espionage Act and that the law violated the First Amendment.[87]

Abrams's case started when a fellow Russian immigrant, Hyman Rosansky, was arrested for dumping leaflets from the roofs of buildings near 2nd Avenue and 8th Street in New York City on August 22, 1918. The leaflets, printed in English and Yiddish, labeled President Wilson a coward and exclaimed, "Awake! Awake, you Workers of the World!"[88] The leaflets claimed that, "America and her Allies have betrayed (the Workers). Their robberish aims are clear to all men."[89] Rosansky gave authorities the names of his colleagues. The leaflets, about five thousand in all, had been printed in a room Abrams rented. Six people were indicted for violating the Espionage Act, though one of the men died before the trial. About a month later, a jury convicted them. The judge allowed Abrams to make a statement on his own behalf but cut him off before he could finish. According to an account of the trial's final day in the *Baltimore American*, Abrams told the court that he "maintained the principles of right and justice" and "if that is a crime, I am proud to be a criminal"—echoing language Goldman had used many times.[90] The judge halted Abrams, reasoning that he would not allow those on trial to "make themselves out as martyrs."[91] When the jury announced its verdict, Abrams's lawyer, the unflappable Weinberger, stood and asked that the conviction be set aside. The judge quickly put a stop to his efforts. He told Weinberger, "This is not time for a soap-box oratory. Sit down. Your clients have been convicted. That is all."[92] As with Debs's trial, Goldman followed what was happening to Abrams

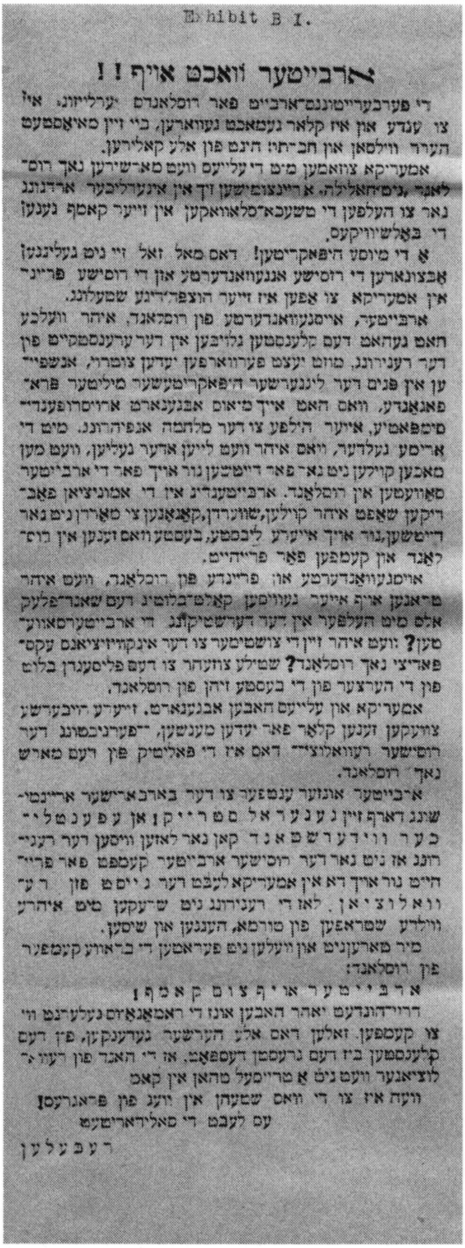

Exhibit B I.

ארבייטער וואכט אויף!!

די פערבערייטונגס־ארבייט פאר רוסלאנדס "ערלייזונג" איז
צו ענדע און איז קלאר געמאכט געווארען, ביי זיין מאיעסטעט
הערר ווילסאן און חבריתו הינם פון אלע קאלירען.
אמעריקא צוזאמען מיט די עלייעס וועט מארשירען נאך רוס־
לאנד ,גיט־חאלילה, א ריינצומישען זיך אין אינערליכער ארדנונג
נאר צו העלפען די טשעכא־סלאוואקען אין זייער קאמף געגען
די באלשעוויקעס.
א די מיוסע היפאקריטען! דאס מאל זאל זיי ניט געלינגען
אבצונארען די רוסישע אנגעווענדערטע און די רוסישע פריינ־
אין אמעריקא צו אפען איז זייער הוצפה'דיגע שמעלונג.
ארבייטער, אימיגראנטען פון רוסלאנד, איהר וועלכע
האט געהאט דעם קלענסטען גלייבען אין דער ערענסטקייט פון
דער רעגירונג, מוזט יעצט פערווארפען יעדען צוטרוי, אנשפיי־
ען אין פנים דער ליגנערישער היפאקריטישער מיליטער פרא־
פאגאנדע, וואס האט אייך מיאוס אבגענארט ארויסרופענדי־
סימפאטיע, אייער הילפע צו דער מלחמה אנפיהרונג. מיט די
אייער געלדער, וואס איהר וועט לייען אדער געליען, וועט מען
מאכען קוילען ניט נאר פאר דייטשען נור אייך פאר די ארבייטער
סאוועטען אין רוסלאנד. ארבייטענדיג אין די אמוניציאן פאב־
ריקען שאפט איהר קוילען, שווערדען, קאנאנען צו מארדען ניט נאר
דייטשען, נור אייך אייערע ליבסטע, בעסטע וואס זענען אין רוס־
לאנד און קעמפען פאר פרייהייט.
אימיגוואנדערטע און פריינדע פון רוסלאנד, וועט איהר
טראגען אויף אייער געוויסען קאלטבלוטיג דעם שאנדפלעק
אלס מיט העלפער אין דער דערשטיקונג די ארבייטערסאווע־
טען? וועט איהר זיין די צושטימער צו דער אינקוויזיציאנס עקס־
פעדיציע נאך רוסלאנד? שטילע צוזעהר צו דעם פליסענדען בלוט
פון די הערצער פון די בעסטע זיהן פון רוסלאנד.
אמעריקא און עלייעס האבען אבגענארט. זייערע היבערישע
צוועקען זענען קלאר פאר יעדען מענשען, "פערניכטונג דער
רוסישער רעוואלוציע" דאס איז די פאליטיק פון דעם מארש
נאך רוסלאנד.
ארבייטער אונזער ענטפער צו דער בארבארישער אריינמי־
שונג דארף זיין ג ע נ ע ר א ל ס ט ר א י ק! און עפענטליכער
ו י ד ע ר ש ט א נ ד קען נאר לאזען וויסען דער רעגי־
רונג אז ניט נאר דער רוסישער ארבייטער קעמפט פאר פריי־
הייט נור אויך דא אין אמעריקא לעבט דער ג א י ס ט פון ר ע־
ו א ל ו צ י א ן. לאז די רעגירונג ניט שיקען מיט איהרע
ווילדע שטראפען פון טורמא, הענגען און שיסען.
מיר מארענעט און וועלען ניט פעראטען די בראווע קעמפער
פון רוסלאנד!
א ר ב י י ט ע ר א ו י ף צ ו ם ק א מ ף!
דרייהונדערט יאהר האבען אונז די ראמאנאוס געלערנט ווי
צו קעמפען. זאלען דאס אלע הערשער געדענקען, פון דעם
קלענסטען ביז דעם גרעסטען דעספאט, אז די האנד פון רעוו־
לוציאנער וועט ניט א טרייסעל טהאן אין קאמ
וועה איז צו די וואס שטעהן אין וועג פון פראגרעס!
עס לעבט די סאלידאריטעט
רעבעלען

Figure 2.4 The Yiddish leaflet associated with the *Abrams v. United States* trial was titled "Workers Wake Up!"

Source: National Archives.

and his co-conspirators. She later wrote that she admired their "brave, determined stand for an ideal's sake."[93]

The Supreme Court took little time in upholding Abrams's conviction, announcing its decision on November 10, 1919. For the first time, justices did not agree in their interpretation of the Espionage Act. In a move that has divided scholars and historians for a century, Justice Holmes, who was joined by Justice Brandeis, wrote one of the Court's most important dissenting opinions. The Court had concluded that Abrams's goal in spreading the leaflets was "to excite, at the supreme crisis of the war, disaffection, sedition, riots, and, as they hoped, revolution."[94] Such a conclusion was sufficient for the majority to once again uphold the Espionage Act. In his dissent, Justice Holmes maintained that the rulings in *Schenck, Debs*, and *Frohwerk* were rightly decided and that Congress has a right to halt messages that are a clear and present danger to the United States.[95] In the final portion, however, he departed substantially from focusing on the law and facts of the case—much like he did in his *Baltzer* draft. Ultimately, Justice Holmes became far more philosophical. In doing so, he wrote one of most important passages in the nation's history regarding freedom of expression:

> When men have realized that time has upset many fighting faiths, they may come to believe even more than they believe the very foundations of their own conduct that the ultimate good desired is better reached by free trade in ideas – that the best test of truth is the power of the thought to get itself accepted in the competition of the market, and that truth is the only ground upon which their wishes safely can be carried out. That at any rate is the theory of our Constitution. It is an experiment, as all life is an experiment. Every year if not every day we have to wager our salvation upon some prophecy based upon imperfect knowledge.[96]

The passage, which by the late 1960s had become the dominant understanding regarding freedom of expression in the United States, introduced the marketplace of ideas metaphor into the Court's vocabulary. Such an approach combines allowing a free exchange of ideas, sans government intervention, with a faith that the truth will emerge and falsity will fail in such a system. Such a system might well have helped Goldman and the many others who protested the war effort during World War I. Rabban labeled Justice Holmes's dissent as the moment when he "joined the postwar civil libertarians."[97] His web of correspondences quickly lauded the dissent. Judge Hand wrote just before Thanksgiving that he "was greatly pleased" and "confident that whether it is avowed or not, in the end your views must prevail after people get over the existing hysteria."[98] Another friend, a philosophy professor, wrote to Justice Holmes that he had "seldom read anything which seemed to me to be so timely and yet of such permanent importance, so courageous and yet so just to all the relevant considerations."[99] Justice Holmes commented in a letter to future Supreme Court Justice Felix Frankfurter, then a law professor at Harvard, that he received some criticism but also praise. Frankfurter reported that he and his colleague Roscoe Pound agreed the "paragraphs will live as long as the Areopagitica," referring to John Milton's seventeenth-century argument for freedom of the press.[100]

Far less clear than the positive response Justice Holmes received were his reasons for dissenting in *Abrams*, contending that the Espionage Act went too far and was not constitutional, after he had written three opinions for a unanimous Court that upheld very similar Espionage Act convictions. The *Abrams* dissent also does not align with his reasoning from *Patterson* about twelve years earlier. It is possible that pressure from his friends and peers—including Judge Hand, Chafee, and Harold Laski, an economics professor who found himself pushed out of Harvard during the period because of his socialist views—were enough to sway him. However, the record of his copious and quite candid correspondences does not include any evidence that he was swayed or changed his mind. In fact, he contended that his dissent in *Abrams* aligned with the other three 1919 decisions.[101]

Rabban concluded that Chafee's landmark article, "Free Speech in War Time," gave Justice Holmes the legal doctrines he needed to support a pro-free expression decision.[102] Other theories suggest the time that had passed since the war's end or the justice's distaste for the cases could have led him to produce a different outcome. Along those lines, in a May 1919 letter to Herbert Croly, a progressive leader and editor for the *New Republic*, Justice Holmes again stated that he "hated to have to write the *Debs* case and still more those of the other poor devils before us."[103] In the same passage, he highlighted that the war was over, then foreshadowed his marketplace of ideas approach when he wrote: "In the main I am for aeration of all effervescing convictions – there is no way so quick for letting them go flat."[104] The dissipating of the pressure the war had placed on the Court and Justice Holmes's long history of seeking to support positions that were in the majority in public opinion provide valid possible explanations for his shift.

Whatever Justice Holmes's reasoning in the *Abrams* dissent, it did not help Goldman. Shortly after the *Abrams* decision was announced, she received her deportation order. Just before Christmas, she was on an Army transport out of the country. The next chapter explores Goldman's activities that led to her deportation.

Notes

1 "Trial and Speeches of Alexander Berkman and Emma Goldman in the United States in District Court, in the City of New York, July 1917" (New York: Mother Earth Publishing Association, 1917), 64, in Candace Falk, with Ronald J. Zboray, et al., eds., *The Emma Goldman Papers: A Microfilm Edition* (Alexandria, VA: Chadwyck-Healey, Inc., 1990; hereafter referred to as Goldman Papers), reel 57.

2 Ibid., 73.

3 David M. Rabban, *Free Speech in the Forgotten Years* (Cambridge: Cambridge University Press, 1997), 2–3. Regarding the counter-majoritarian difficulty, see Alexander Bickel, *The Least Dangerous Branch: The Supreme Court at the Bar of Politics* (New Haven, CT: Yale University Press, 1986), 16–23; Barry Friedman, "The History of the Countermajoritarian Difficulty, Part One: The Road to Judicial Supremacy," *New York University Law Review* 73 (1998): 334–335.

4 See *Barron v. Baltimore*, 32 U.S. 243 (1833). The Court concluded that John Barron, whose wharf-related business was damaged when the city dumped massive amounts of sand in the harbor, did not have a legitimate Fifth Amendment claim against Baltimore because the amendment was only intended to limit the federal government's power. Thus, the promises of the Bill of Rights did not extend to the states.

5 U.S. Const. amend XIV, § 1 reads: "All persons born or naturalized in the United States and subject to the jurisdiction thereof, are citizens of the United States and of the State wherein they reside. No State shall make or enforce any law which shall abridge the privileges or immunities of citizens of the United States; nor shall any State deprive any person of life, liberty, or property, without due process of law; nor deny to any person within its jurisdiction the equal protection of the laws."

6 *The Slaughter-House Cases*, 83 U.S. 36, 82 (1873).

7 See *Near v. Minnesota*, 283 U.S. 697 (1931).

8 Mark Graber, *Transforming Free Speech: The Ambiguous Legacy of Civil Libertarianism* (Berkeley, CA: University of California Press, 1991), 50.

9 Rabban, *Free Speech in the Forgotten Years*, 2.

10 *Dred Scott v. Sandford*, 60 U.S. 393, 454 (1857).

11 Abraham Lincoln, "Speech on the Dred Scott Decision" (speech, Springfield, IL, June 26, 1857), University of Virginia, www.virginia.edu/woodson/courses/aas-hius366a/lincoln.html.

12 Charles Evan Hughes, *The Supreme Court of the United States: Its Foundations, Methods, and Achievements: An Interpretation* (New York: Columbia University Press, 1966), 50.

13 *Ex parte Merryman*, 17 F. Cas. 144 (C.C.D. Md. 1861).

14 Keith E. Wittington, *The Political Foundations of Judicial Supremacy: The Presidency, the Supreme Court, and Constitutional Leadership in U.S. History* (Princeton, NJ: Princeton University Press, 2007), 28.

15 Alexander Hamilton, "The Federalist No. 78: The Judiciary Department," www.congress.gov/resources/display/content/The+Federalist+Papers#TheFederalistPapers-78. Hamilton emphasized, "The judiciary, on the

contrary, has no influence over either the sword or the purse; no direction either of the strength or of the wealth of the society; and can take no active resolution whatever."

16 Robert G. McCloskey, *The American Supreme Court* (Chicago: University of Chicago Press, 2010), 91.

17 McCloskey, *The American Supreme Court*, 85–89; Lewis F. Powell, "'Carolene Products' Revisited," *Columbia Law Review* 82, 6 (1982): 1089.

18 Spencer first articulated the theory of Social Darwinism in *Principles of Biology* (London: Williams & Norgate, 1864). For more on its American influence, see Mike Hawkins, *Social Darwinism in European and American Thought, 1860–1945: Nature and Model and Nature as Threat* (Cambridge, UK: Cambridge University Press, 1997); Richard Hofstadter, *Social Darwinism in American Thought* (Boston: Beacon Press, 1992).

19 *Lochner v. New York*, 198 U.S. 45, 75 (1905) (Holmes, J., dissenting).

20 Ibid., 52, 64. For more on *Lochner*'s legacy, see Cass R. Sunstein, "Lochner's Legacy," *Columbia Law Review* 87, 5 (1987): 873–919; Powell, "'Carolene Products' Revisited," 1089; Erwin Chemerinsky, "The Supreme Court and the Fourteenth Amendment: The Unfulfilled Promise," *Loyola of Los Angeles Law Review* 25 (1991): 1150.

21 *Lochner*, 198 U.S. at 75 (Holmes, J., dissenting).

22 Sunstein, "Lochner's Legacy," 874; Robert Kerr, "Naturalizing the Artificial Citizen: Repeating *Lochner*'s Error in *Citizen's United v. Federal Election Commission*," *Communication Law & Policy* 15, 4 (2010): 311–363; Michael Klarman, *From Jim Crow to Civil Rights: The Supreme Court and the Struggle for Racial Equality* (Oxford, UK: Oxford University Press, 2004), 23.

23 *The Slaughter-House Cases*, 83 U.S. 36, 82 (1873), represent the most famous precedent in this regard. The Court ruled that the "equal protection" clause of the Fourteenth Amendment did not apply to private property and that it only came into play in instances that involved national citizenship, not legal questions regarding state laws.

24 *United States v. E.C. Knight*, 156 U.S. 1, 11–12 (1895).

25 *Hammer v. Dagenhart*, 247 U.S. 251, 275 (1918).

26 McCloskey, *The American Supreme Court*, 97.

27 *Child Labor Tax Case*, 259 U.S. 20, 43 (1922).

28 *Adkins v. Children's Hospital*, 261 U.S. 525 (1923). The precedent was ultimately overturned in *West Coast Hotel v. Parrish*, 300 U.S. 379 (1937).

29 William Lasser, "The Supreme Court in Periods of Critical Realignment," *Journal of Politics* 47, 4 (1985): 1182–1985; Jeffrey Segal and Harold Spaeth, *The Supreme Court and the Attitudinal Model Revisited* (Cambridge: Cambridge University Press, 2005), 139.

30 Rabban, *Free Speech in the Forgotten Years*, 18.

31 Act of June 15, 1917, ch. 30, 40 *Stat* 217.

32 Margaret Blanchard, *Revolutionary Sparks: Freedom of Expression in Modern America* (New York: Oxford University Press, 1992), 72.

33 Blanchard, *Revolutionary Sparks,* 75; Harold L. Nelson, *Freedom of the Press from Hamilton to the Warren Court* (Indianapolis: Bobbs-Merrill, 1967), xxxiii; Rabban, *Free Speech in the Forgotten Years*, 75.

34 Blanchard, *Revolutionary Sparks,* 75–76; Thomas F. Carroll, "Freedom of Speech and Press in War Time: The Espionage Act," *Michigan Law Review* 17, 8 (1919): 629–636; Donald Johnson, "Wilson, Burleson, and Censorship in the First World War," *Journal of Southern History* 28, 1 (1962): 46–58; Nelson, *Freedom of the Press*, xxxiii–xxxv; Geoffrey R. Stone, "Judge Learned Hand and the Espionage Act of 1917: A Mystery Unraveled," *University of Chicago Law Review* 70, 1 (2003): 335–358.
35 Act of May 16, 1918, ch. 76, 40 *Stat* 553. See also Blanchard, *Revolutionary Sparks*, 77; Sheldon M. Novick, "The Unrevised Holmes and Freedom of Expression," *The Supreme Court Review* 1991 (1991): 330.
36 *Patterson v. Colorado*, 205 U.S. 454 (1907). For another example, see *Fox v. Washington*, 236 U.S. 273 (1915).
37 *Patterson*, 205 U.S. at 459.
38 Ibid.
39 Rabban, *Free Speech in the Forgotten Years*, 132–133.
40 Jeffrey Rosen, *The Supreme Court: The Personalities and Rivalries that Defined American* (New York: Times Books/Henry Holt and Company, 2007), 73.
41 Ibid.
42 *Patterson v. Colorado*, 205 U.S. 454, 465 (1907) (Harlan, J., dissenting).
43 Rabban, *Free Speech in the Forgotten Years*, 1.
44 "30 Germans Are Arrested in South Dakota for Opposing the War and the Draft Law," *New York Times*, August 28, 1917.
45 Novick, "Unrevised Holmes," 331.
46 *Schenck v. United States*, 249 U.S. 47, 50–51 (1919).
47 "Socialists Guilty of Opposing Draft," *Philadelphia Inquirer*, December 21, 1917.
48 Novick, "Unrevised Holmes," 304–305.
49 *Selective Draft Law Cases*, 245 U.S. 366 (1918).
50 *Goldman & Berkman v. United States*: Assignments of Error, July 17, 1917, Goldman Papers, reel 57; *Goldman & Berkman v. United States*: Brief for Plaintiffs, November 30, 1917, 33–40, Goldman Papers, reel 59.
51 *Goldman & Berkman* Brief, 8–24.
52 Ibid., 20–21.
53 *Selective Draft Law Cases*, 245 U.S. 366, 390 (1918).
54 *Goldman v. United States*, 245 U.S. 474, 475–477 (1918); *Selective Draft Law Cases.*
55 Novick, "Unrevised Holmes," 389. Since this is an unpublished decision, no official record of it exists in the court's archives. *Baltzer v. United States*, 248 U.S. 593 (1918) includes one sentence: "Judgment reversed, upon confession of error; and cause remanded for further proceedings in accordance with law."
56 Novick, "Unrevised Holmes," 389.
57 Ibid.
58 Ibid.
59 *Abrams v. United States*, 250 U.S. 616, 624–631 (1919) (Holmes, J., dissenting).

60 Novick, "Unrevised Holmes," 332.
61 Ibid.
62 Ibid., 331.
63 Emma Goldman, "To All My Dear Ones," *Mother Earth Bulletin*, April 1918, 1.
64 *United States v. Schenck*, 253 F. 212 (E.D. Pa.1918).
65 Emma Goldman, *Living My Life* (Garden City, NY: Garden City Publishing, 1934), 220–221; "Debs Arrested; Sedition Charged," *New York Times*, July 1, 1918.
66 Eugene V. Debs, "Canton Speech" (speech, Canton, OH, June 16, 1918), *Ayers Primary Sources*, http://college.cengage.com/history/ayers_primary_sources/eugene_cantonspeech_1918.htm
67 Ibid.
68 "Debs Denies Nothing in His Pleas to Jury," *Cleveland Plain Dealer*, September 12, 1918.
69 Ibid. See also Alice Wexler, *Emma Goldman: An Intimate Life* (New York: Pantheon Books, 1984), 257.
70 Kenneth Ward and Aimee Edmondson, "The Espionage Conviction of Kansas City Editor Jacob Frohwerk: 'A Clear and Present Danger' to the United States," *Journal of Media Law & Ethics* 6, 1/2 (Summer/Fall 2017): 39–56.
71 *Schenck v. United States*, 249 U.S. 47, 52 (1919).
72 U.S. Const. amend. I.
73 *Schenck*, 249 U.S. at 52.
74 Ibid.
75 Holmes to Harold Laski, March 16, 1919, in *The Essential Holmes*, ed. Richard A. Posner (Chicago: University of Chicago Press, 1992), 316.
76 Ibid.
77 Zechariah Chafee, "Freedom of Speech in War Time," *Harvard Law Review* 32, 8 (1919): 942.
78 Ibid., 943–944.
79 *Masses v. Patten*, 244 F. 535, 544 (S.D.N.Y, 1917).
80 Louis Menand, *The Metaphysical Club: A Story of Ideas in America* (New York: Farrar, Straus & Giroux, 2002), 424–425.
81 *Masses* 244 F. at 540.
82 Chafee, "Freedom of Speech in War Time," 962.
83 Menand, *The Metaphysical Club*, 427.
84 Oliver Wendell Holmes to Learned Hand, June 24, 1918, Oliver Wendell Holmes Jr. Digital Suite, Harvard Law Library.
85 Oliver Wendell Holmes to Learned Hand, February 25, 1919, Oliver Wendell Holmes Jr. Digital Suite, Harvard Law Library.
86 Oliver Wendell Holmes to Learned Hand, April 3, 1919, Oliver Wendell Holmes Jr. Digital Suite, Harvard Law Library.
87 *Abrams v. United States*, 250 U.S. 616, 617–618 (1919).
88 Ibid., 620.
89 Ibid., 621.
90 "Five Anarchists Get Long Terms," *Baltimore American*, October 26, 1918.

91 Ibid.
92 "Oratory at End of Trial Halted," *San Diego Union*, October 24, 1918.
93 Goldman, *Living My Life*, 666.
94 *Abrams*, 623.
95 Ibid., 627 (Holmes, J., dissenting).
96 Ibid., 630 (Holmes, J., dissenting).
97 Rabban, *Free Speech in the Forgotten Years*, 342.
98 Learned Hand to Oliver Wendell Holmes, November 25, 1919, Oliver Wendell Holmes Jr. Digital Suite, Harvard Law Library.
99 Morris Cohen to Oliver Wendell Holmes, December 4, 1919, Oliver Wendell Holmes Jr. Digital Suite, Harvard Law Library.
100 Felix Frankfurter to Oliver Wendell Holmes, November 26, 1919, Oliver Wendell Holmes Jr. Digital Suite, Harvard Law Library. Frankfurter, who was an adviser to President Woodrow Wilson at the Paris Peace Conference that year, helped found the American Civil Liberties Union in 1920; he joined the Supreme Court in 1939.
101 Menand, *The Metaphysical Club*, 430.
102 Rabban, *Free Speech in the Forgotten Years*, 7.
103 Oliver Wendell Holmes to Herbert Croly, May 12, 1919, Oliver Wendell Holmes Jr. Digital Suite, Harvard Law Library. Holmes marked, in underline, "private" at the top of the letter. He ended the letter in the same way, writing "of course it is only for your private eye."
104 Ibid.

3 Goldman, *Mother Earth*, and the No-Conscription League

Goldman's arrest in 1917 under the Selective Service Act was not her first brush with the law. She was arrested numerous times, most famously in connection with President William McKinley's assassination after the man who killed him said Goldman's words inspired him. Goldman's life in America also included an animated public debate with Anthony Comstock, the postal inspector who championed an act giving the postal service the power to destroy any mail they found indecent or obscene. Beyond these examples, Goldman also became involved with the Free Speech League and at times worked with birth control advocate Margaret Sanger. In short, she was already a household name to many in the United States when she was arrested for protesting the draft. This chapter examines pertinent details such as these from Goldman's life before her arrest and conviction in federal court.

The chapter also includes an analysis of *Mother Earth*, Goldman's anarchist magazine, which, along with a tireless public-speaking schedule, was one of Goldman's main ways of sharing her views. *Mother Earth* was particularly important to Goldman's No-Conscription League efforts and was used as evidence against her in federal court. This chapter explores the writings and speeches Goldman and her allies used to promote the No-Conscription League's principles, which would later lead to Goldman's arrest and deportation.

The Rise of "Red Emma"

One incident struck such a chord with Goldman that it defined her lifelong course. Chicago anarchists staged a peaceful protest in May 1886 after Pinkerton police shot striking workers at the McCormick Harvesting Plant. After police intervened, the Haymarket Square protest turned violent and eight officers died, instigating a city-wide hunt for immigrant radicals. Courts convicted eight anarchist leaders of murder, even though six of them were not at the protest.[1] Their conviction and November 1887 execution upset Goldman's certainty about

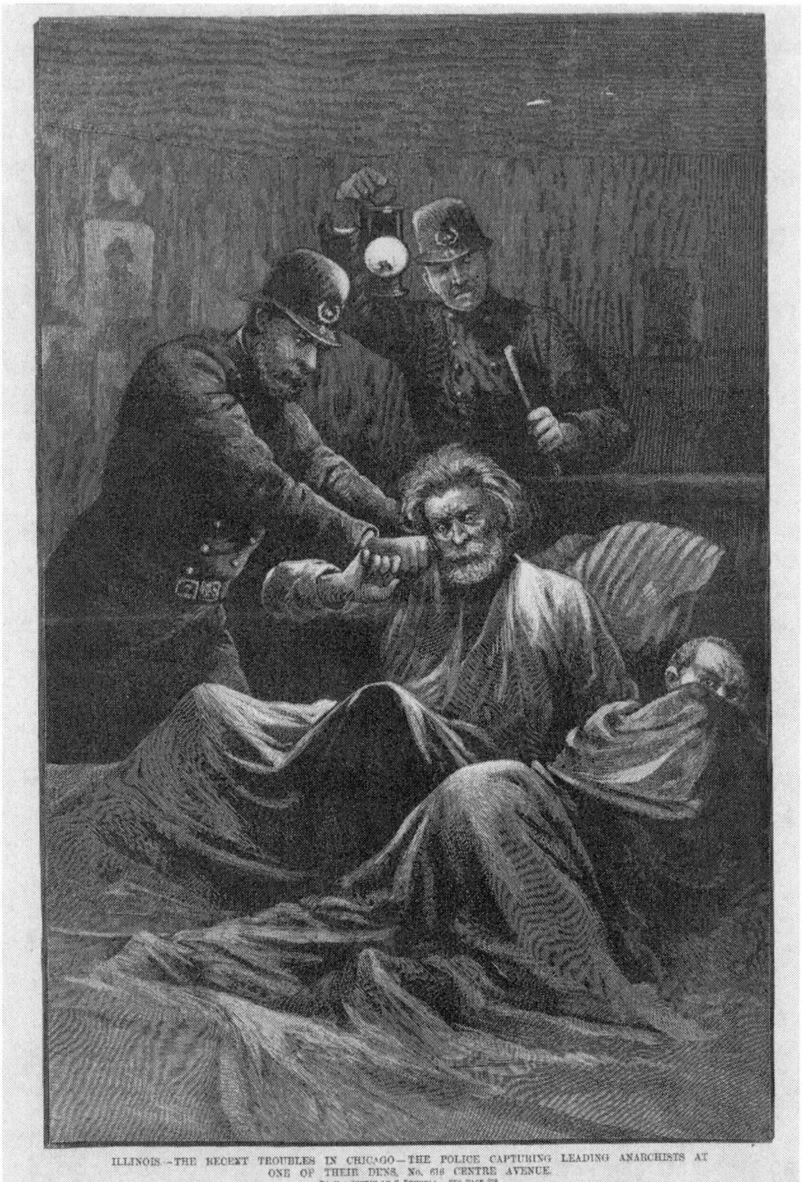

Figure 3.1 An illustration from *Frank Leslie's Weekly* shows authorities capturing "leading anarchists in one of their dens" following the Haymarket riot.

Source: Library of Congress.

the sanctity of free speech and drove her to anarchism; she explained that it ignited "a burning faith, a determination to dedicate myself to the memory of my martyred comrades, to make their case my own, to make known to the world their beautiful lives and heroic deaths."[2] It affected her for the rest of her life; though she died in Toronto in 1940, she was buried near the Haymarket rioters in Chicago.[3]

Soon after Haymarket, Goldman moved from Rochester to New York City's Jewish immigrant district and worked as a seamstress while she immersed herself in studying anarchy. Goldman wrote in her memoir that she arrived in New York City with five dollars, her sewing machine, and the addresses of an aunt and *Freiheit*, Johann Most's German anarchist paper.[4] She became a disciple of Most, leader of the European immigrant anarchist movement, who eventually urged her to train as a public speaker. Most sent Goldman on her first speaking tour in 1890.[5] More significantly, in New York City Goldman met her closest confidante Berkman, with whom she eventually developed an anarchist commune.[6] According to biographer Kenneth Wenzer, the pair had identical philosophies, shaped not only by their time and treatment in the United States but also by a number of Russian and Judaic writers.[7] Goldman later incorporated additional ideals that she absorbed while studying to be a midwife in Europe.[8] Goldman's version of anarchy promoted autonomy, liberty, social cooperation, individual initiative, meaningful work, and free love; she thoroughly opposed centralized authority, censorship, and coercion.[9]

Given their sympathy for the largely immigrant working class, labor strikes especially moved Goldman and Berkman.[10] One led Berkman to attempt an assassination of Carnegie Steel Chairman Henry Clay Frick in 1892. Goldman and Berkman both were enraged by the "slaughter of steel-workers," including a young boy, by Pinkertons at one of Frick's mills. Berkman hatched the idea to punish Frick for the "wonton murders," but Goldman vowed to help by raising funds for Berkman's trip to Pennsylvania and articulating the meaning of his actions to the nation's labor force.[11] The press instantly charged Goldman with conspiracy; she noted that the newspapers had scarcely mentioned her before but now attached her name every day to the "most sensational stories."[12] A month later, the *New York World* singled Goldman out in an article that labeled her the queen of the anarchists and Berkman as her tool.[13] Wenzer argued that the incident "permanently fixed in the minds of Americans the foreignness of Goldman and Berkman."[14]

During Berkman's incarceration, Goldman became a leader of the anarcho-communist movement and increased her public speaking, using the anarchist message in part to defend her comrade. More commonly, though, she encouraged her working-class audiences to take direct action

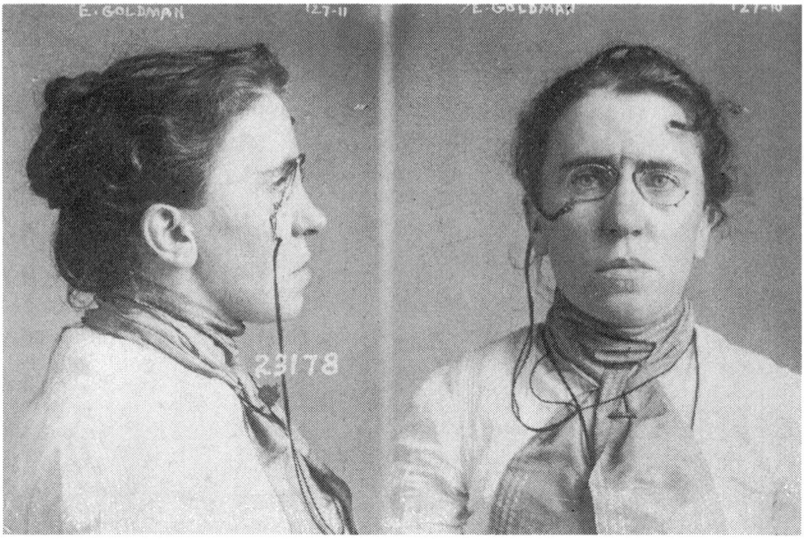

Figure 3.2 Goldman spent ten months in jail in 1893 for a New York speech urging workers to improve their condition.

Source: Library of Congress.

and improve their economic condition.[15] In one particularly famous speech at an 1893 rally of unemployed New Yorkers, she removed her red-flowered hat, rolled up her sleeves, and shouted in German, "Become daring enough to demand your rights. Demonstrate before the palaces of the rich. Demand work. If they do not give you work, demand bread. If they deny you both, take bread. It is your sacred right."[16] Newspapers teemed with accusations that Goldman aimed to agitate immigrants to insurrection, looting, and even murder.[17] Authorities arrested her as she arrived to speak at a similar rally in Philadelphia two days later, charging her with inciting to riot. Goldman described her trial as a "farce," with witnesses delivering false testimony of her cries for "revolution, violence, and bloodshed."[18] On the basis of those reports, the judge found Goldman guilty, despite her arguments that her addresses simply represented a use of her right to free speech and she had done nothing unlawful.[19] Though the verdict further embittered Goldman against the state, she considered her ten-month imprisonment a blessing because she discovered her own strength and will to fight for her ideals.[20]

Newly emboldened, Goldman returned to lecturing immediately upon her release. Among the many who heard her speak throughout the country was Polish-American steel worker Leon Czolgosz, who went on to assassinate President McKinley in 1901. Czolgosz's actions—and his claims that Goldman inspired him—swelled public opinion against anarchists.[21] Headlines reporting the crime accused Goldman of inciting Czolgosz, and people in the streets buzzing over the assassination labeled Goldman a beast and a bloodthirsty monster.[22] Goldman had just stepped out of the bath at a friend's home in Chicago when police came through a window to arrest her for conspiracy. Authorities held Goldman for a month under suspicion for the assassination, but they never charged her.[23] After her arrest, the *Washington Post* quoted her as saying that Czolgosz was

> one of those downtrodden men who see all the misery which the rich inflict upon the poor; who think of it, who brood over it, and then, in despair, resolve to strike a great blow, as they think, for the good of their fellow men.[24]

She also wrote in an article for *Free Society* that she sympathized with the accused assassin, whom the public had denounced as a foreigner even though he was born in America. She believed Czolgosz carried out his violent act because he could not bear to witness the misery and suffering of his peers, imposed in part by a greedy and despotic president. "The blame for such acts," she wrote, "must be laid at the door of those who are responsible for the injustice and humanity which dominate the world."[25] Five years later, Goldman devoted part of the October 1906 issue of her magazine *Mother Earth* to essays marking the anniversary of Czolgosz's execution, which she labeled a tragedy. The tone of the essays echoed Goldman's sentiments half a decade earlier, calling McKinley corrupt and Czolgosz's motives pure.[26]

Goldman's sympathy for Czolgosz did nothing to endear her to the American public. These incidents and their newspaper coverage—much of which demonized Goldman—increased her notoriety to the point that mothers frightened children into eating their vegetables by threatening that "Red Emma" would get them if they didn't.[27] The notoriety led to more lecture invitations. Despite a new wave of xenophobia following McKinley's assassination, the Progressive movement increasingly drew an audience of American-born, middle-class radicals to hear Goldman's reform messages; Goldman believed everyone could work together toward the same ends.[28] Goldman's relationship with physician/activist Ben Reitman further enlarged her audiences. Her manager as well as her lover, Reitman deftly used his management and public relations skills to secure venues ranging from underground mine shafts to Carnegie Hall and attract spectators totaling 50,000–75,000 per year.[29]

Mother Earth as an Anarchist Forum

Goldman sought an even wider audience with her magazine, founded in 1906. Its office—which doubled as her apartment—also became the central hub for New York City's anarchist movement. Biographer Alice Wexler asserted that *Mother Earth* quickly became Goldman's identity, allowing her to devote all her time to anarchist writing and lecturing.[30] The two sustained each other; *Mother Earth* promoted, published, and reported on Goldman's lectures, and Goldman funneled funds collected on the speaking circuit into her magazine. She also distributed copies of the magazine at her appearances. In addition to Goldman's work, the monthly periodical contained essays from other anarchists on contemporary issues as well as excerpts from writers who inspired the anarchist movement.[31] By promoting female sexuality, independence, equality, and access to birth control, *Mother Earth* also demonstrated the effect of anarchy on feminism.[32]

Goldman later wrote that *Mother Earth* represented the culmination of years of work. Whereas the spoken word was "fleeting at best," printed thought was "more lasting in its effect." She surmised that her journal would be "a place of expression for the young idealists in art and letters," a place where she predicted—albeit incorrectly—they could "speak without censor."[33] Goldman thought of the name for her periodical as she walked on a farm and noticed "life germinating in the womb of Mother Earth." It occurred to her that *Mother Earth* would be an appropriate name for a publication intended to be a "nourisher of man, man freed and unhindered in his access to the free earth."[34] The introductory essay issued an invitation for oppressed people to take back what was theirs. It averred that when America's forefathers first arrived, Mother Earth had extended "her inviting and hospitable arms to all those who came to her from arbitrary and despotic lands," ready to "give herself alike to all her children." However, Goldman continued, a few corrupt individuals seized the land and stripped it of its freedom, becoming dependent on possessions, wealth, and power. "A period of but a hundred years had sufficed to turn a great republic, once gloriously established, into an arbitrary state which subdued a vast number of its people into material and intellectual slavery," she wrote. *Mother Earth* strove to appeal to all who opposed encroachment on public and individual lives. It promised "the tender shade of a new dawn for a humanity free from the dread of want, the dread of starvation."[35]

The compiler of a *Mother Earth* anthology, Peter Glassgold argued that Goldman's magazine was among the best written and best produced anarchist publications. Because of its quality as well as its political neutrality, it developed a broad readership, appealing not only to anarchists but also to "socialists, single-taxers, militant Wobblies, social reformers, and even parlor liberals."[36] The mainstream press quickly took notice; within a month of the first issue, the *New York Times* began mentioning the magazine in reports of Goldman's appearances.[37] Articles noting Berkman's May 1906 release from prison for his attempt on Frick's life inaugurated the habit of quoting essays from the periodical as evidence of Goldman's ideals, unwittingly offering *Mother Earth* free publicity and broadening the reach of its contents.[38]

Fights for Free Speech

The more popular Goldman became, the more authorities and detractors targeted her. Police often disrupted and forcibly dispersed her appearances, and they arrested her multiple times.[39] Thus, Goldman developed a disdain for law enforcement. After one "brutal and unspeakable" attack on free speech by New York police, Goldman wrote in *Mother Earth* that "we should long since have placed a club instead of a torch in the hand of the Goddess of Liberty—the police mace is not merely the symbol, but the very essence of our 'liberty and order.'"[40] Goldman detailed in *Mother Earth* several attacks on her own speech, but she also engaged in vigorous fights for others' free expression. In addition to legal proceedings, Goldman wrote articles, staged free-speech protests, and organized local free-speech committees.[41]

The Free Speech League became the first organization in the United States to support freedom of expression, regardless of viewpoint, when it formed in 1902 in New York.[42] Goldman joined forces with the league after authorities arrested British anarchist John Turner under the Immigration Act of 1903, or as Goldman called it, the "Federal Anti-Anarchist Law."[43] The Free Speech League secured famous attorney Clarence Darrow to represent Turner before the Supreme Court and raised funds for his defense. Furthermore, Goldman engaged in a public crusade on Turner's behalf. She knew the court would uphold his deportation, and it did—dismissing his attorney's First Amendment-based claims. However, Goldman felt her campaign would bring the "absurd" immigration law to the public's attention and "awaken many Americans to the fact that the liberties guaranteed in the United States… had become nothing but empty phrases to be used as fire-crackers on the Fourth of July."[44]

Goldman nearly fell victim to the Immigration Act herself in 1909. The Free Speech League came to her aid, helping her file suit against Philadelphia officials who refused to let her speak, but the suit was unsuccessful. When the Pennsylvania court ruled that "anarchist alien" Goldman could not claim legal protection for speech that defied the government, judges noted that under the 1903 law, she could be deported.[45] A Free Speech League address published in *Mother Earth* the next month implored authorities to merely ignore anarchists' speech if they did not like it; "let them not endeavor to close our mouths by the strong hand." The statement encouraged the public to take up the free speech cause and put down tyranny, demanding the right of free expression even for "the most hated" individuals.[46]

Though the public usually derided Goldman, the Free Speech League's support of her cause seemed to rally opinion to her side. Free speech advocate Alden Freeman compiled examples of public support for Goldman's right to speak into a pamphlet entitled "The Fight for Free Speech." Freeman anonymously quoted letters from throughout the country, written by everyone from laborers to eminent citizens, applauding the Free Speech League's efforts to support Goldman's right to speak—even if they did not agree with her.[47] The issue awakened some of America's privileged to the plight of immigrants and laborers, such as one woman who wrote a letter to the Philadelphia *Public Ledger*. A descendent of the nation's first settlers and many who had fought in wars waged for American freedom, the woman wrote that she was not an anarchist but went to hear Goldman speak so she could learn about "what Miss Goldman calls anarchism." The menacing police presence shocked the woman. "It was the first time in my life I was conscious of tyranny," the woman wrote. "It was the first time in my life as an American woman I felt outraged, instead of protected, by the Government of my country."[48] The *Ledger* and others in the press sided with Goldman in the dispute as well, to some extent. The *Burlington* (Vermont) *Daily News* reprinted several articles questioning why Philadelphia silenced Goldman, all declaring that the Constitution protected her right to speak. However, they also took jabs at Goldman, arguing that barring her speech only increased her popularity and made her a martyr; if she had just been allowed to speak, she would have talked herself out, and no one would have been affected by her "nonsense."[49] Other newspaper articles, such as one in the *Harrisburg* (Pennsylvania) *Daily Independent*, expressed that the courts did not go far enough. The Harrisburg writer applauded the judge's verdict that anarchist speech should be stifled but questioned why Goldman and other anarchists still were allowed to circulate the printed word, which had much greater reach.[50]

Authorities stifled Goldman's speech even when she wasn't preaching anarchy because some thought her subject was obscene; New York City police arrested her under the Comstock Law for lecturing on preventing pregnancy. The birth control issue fit Goldman's anarchist ideology because she believed women bearing multiple children added to the woes of the lower class. As a midwife, Goldman saw first-hand the "fierce, blind struggle of the women of the poor against frequent pregnancies." She lamented that having a larger brood of children than a father's wage could afford made each child a curse. In her memoir, Goldman relayed the tale of a woman who already had eight children, four of whom had died in infancy. "The remaining were sickly and undernourished, like most of the ill-born, ill-kept, and unwanted children who trailed at my feet when I was helping another poor creature into the world," Goldman wrote. She concluded that women and children carried "the heaviest burden of our ruthless economic system."[51] Goldman had begun lecturing on the need to limit offspring in 1900 as one of many subjects related to the social struggle, but she did not discuss specific methods. After pioneering birth control advocate and eventual Planned Parenthood founder Margaret Sanger faced problems under the Comstock Law, Goldman resolved to take up the cause in earnest.[52] Goldman and Sanger met after Sanger moved to New York in 1911, and Goldman supported Sanger's birth control campaign.[53] After federal authorities charged Sanger and her husband with distributing obscene materials, Goldman came to their aid by collecting funds for their defense and crusading on their behalf, via lectures and in *Mother Earth.* One essay Goldman published avowed that if everyone who believed in practicing prevention voiced their opinions "openly and loudly, there would be such a volume of indignation against the persecution of Margaret Sanger that the government would not dare railroad her to prison." Goldman called on readers to contact *Mother Earth* or the Free Speech League to support Sanger's work.[54]

Another essay on the Sanger case lashed out at Anthony Comstock, "the self-appointed censor of our morals," calling his actions insolent and his law absurd and antiquated.[55] This was not the first time that *Mother Earth* attacked Comstock. Labeled by one historian as "the foremost policeman of private vices in America's Gilded Age," Comstock formed the New York Society for Suppression of Vice and lobbied Congress for a federal obscenity statute. As a special agent of the U.S. Post Office, Comstock spent more than four decades policing the mail, seizing material he deemed immoral, and arresting thousands under what came to be known as the Comstock Law.[56] Passed in March 1873, the act's purpose was to prevent the mail from being used to corrupt the public. It specifically banned materials promoting contraception and abortion, though Comstock targeted all sorts of literature and art that he considered obscene.[57] Goldman took multiple jabs at Comstock in the very first issue of *Mother Earth.* In the introductory essay, she asserted that journalists in the United States faced censors far more powerful than those in Russia, including Comstock. Furthermore, she published a full essay on "Comstockery" and its "deplorable" originator.[58] The second *Mother Earth* issue contained a short dig declaring that Comstock was "the grim angel who drove Adam and Eve out of

Figure 3.3 Emma Goldman in 1911, the year she met birth control advocate Margaret Sanger.

Source: Library of Congress.

Paradise"—directly above a quote alluding to the need for birth control: "As long as there are women who must fear to become mothers on account of economic difficulties or moral prejudices, the emancipation of woman is only a phrase."[59] Comstock held up delivery of the January 1910 *Mother Earth* because Goldman's article entitled "White Slave Traffic" mentioned prostitution, leading to more complaints against the postal inspector in the periodical.[60]

Finally, in 1916, the Comstock Law landed Goldman in jail. Authorities picked her up on February 11 as she attempted to enter Forward Hall in New York City to speak on atheism; they charged her for lecturing on birth control three days earlier. Goldman wrote in an open letter to the press that she was "taken to a filthy station house, then hustled into a patrol wagon, rushed to the Clinton Street jail, there searched in the most vulgar manner." She attributed "the whole brutality of the New York police" to their disagreement with her anarchist beliefs, and she implored that editors set aside their similar prejudices against her to present the facts to their readers. Though Comstock himself had died, she wrote, his successor was "leaving nothing undone" to make intelligent conversation about birth control impossible. She averred that she did not disseminate knowledge on the subject to be lewd but because "the desperate condition" of workers warranted it. She declared that "the only way to get rid of the law is to awaken the public to the fact that it has outlived its purposes," and she would be glad to go to jail if that would help wipe it out.[61] Goldman hoped her letter would encourage the newspapers to promote a protest meeting planned for March 1 at Carnegie Hall; she wrote to a friend that the *New York Globe* ran the letter in its entirety and the *New York Tribune* had one paragraph, but others ignored it.[62] The newspapers spread her message in coverage published after the meeting, though, describing the protest as a "huge gathering" that filled the hall to the rafters. The New York *Sun* identified Goldman as an anarchist and emphasized her defiance of the law, including her pledge that even if she went to jail, she would come out still speaking about birth control.[63] Goldman repeated her pledge in two April 1916 *Mother Earth* essays, written while she awaited trial. "I never will acquiesce or submit to authority, nor will I make peace with a system which degrades women to a mere incubator and which fattens on her innocent victims," she vowed. "I now and here declare war upon this system and shall not rest until the path has been cleared for a free motherhood and a healthy, joyous and happy childhood."[64]

Goldman also used the courtroom as a forum for promoting birth control and calling for a repeal of the law barring the dissemination of information about preventing pregnancy. She spoke for an hour, concluding that if working for a healthy motherhood and happy childhood were crimes, then she was proud to be a criminal. The judge pronounced her guilty and sentenced her to fifteen days in jail, but again, Goldman considered her sentence a blessing. She believed that her arrest and that of many others for the same crime had achieved her aim of raising awareness on the birth control issue, advancing the cause "at least ten years."[65] Furthermore, Goldman believed her fight for the rights of women doubled as a "fight in behalf of freedom of speech and press on the great social problems of our time."[66] One of those social problems was war—another issue about which Goldman soon had an opportunity to speak from a courtroom.

Goldman's Anti-War Stance

Goldman wrote in her autobiography that the excitement of the birth-control campaign did not detract from the important issue of war: "The European slaughter was continuing, and the American militarists were growing bloodthirsty at the smell of the red stream."[67] From the start of World War I in 1914, *Mother Earth* contained articles opposing the conflict, noting that "the murderous blast" for the sake of capitalism contradicted anarchist values of human life, social liberty, international brotherhood, and the economic interests of the working class.[68] The May 1915 *Mother Earth* contained a manifesto that expanded on anarchists' reasons for opposition, emphasizing the inevitability of the barbaric war due to a flawed social system, "founded on the exploitation of the workers," that "compels Labor to submit to the domination of a minority of parasites who hold both political and economic power." The people, argued the manifesto, had entrusted the State to keep peace, but the government deliberately betrayed them. Thus, the manifesto declared, anarchists must encourage the people to revolt and win complete freedom, doing away with war and militarism forever.[69]

As war continued in Europe, articles against the remote conflict appeared in *Mother Earth* periodically, often focusing on soldiers pressed into battle against their will. One listed the fallacies of war, including the myth that militarism produces courage. The essay's writer did not perceive courage when "one is taken by the neck and forced into the army" and then "pressed forward by the mass behind, with, as is often the case, officers in the rear with revolvers to shoot those who may hesitate." The author concluded that instead of courage, forced enlistment demonstrated compulsion.[70] Another article criticized war propagandists for lulling the naïve into believing their countries were fighting for liberty "when all of them seize upon the individual like ghouls greedy for human flesh, entrain him like an animal...and send him to the slaughter."[71] At least one essay combined war protest with promotion of birth control. Penned by "A Mother of Seven Children," the article declared, "I claim every mother should refuse to bring children into the world to be used as targets for the cannon." The mother insisted that none of her three sons should be forced to fight other people's battles. She concluded, "This no doubt is one of the reasons the fighters of Birth Control are so active; they realize without our babies they couldn't go far with war."[72]

Mother Earth increased its war dissent when it became clear the United States would get involved. Goldman later wrote that she could not give up the anti-war stance she'd held for twenty-five years just because President Wilson "had ceased to be 'too proud' to let American boys do the fighting, while he and other statesmen remained at home."[73] In the March 1917 *Mother Earth*, she called for "every liberty-loving person to voice a fiery protest against the participation of this country in the European mass murder." She believed that Americans, having seen the devastation that the war had wrought in Europe, never would support it. She denied the war brought freedom; no one would benefit from it but the "exploiters" who "coined huge fortunes" out of "the misery of the people." She criticized Wilson for claiming to want peace then supplying the war effort with munitions and food stuffs, feeding the "fires of war" while starving the American people. She urged Americans to tell the greedy profiteers they could fight their own wars; the laborers would not do it for them. They would not kill, she famously argued, nor lend themselves to be killed.[74]

A Manifesto Against Conscription

The March 1917 article revealed Goldman's feelings about conscription; she insisted that it had "destroyed every vestige of liberty in Europe," for those forced into military service lost all power to act voluntarily.[75] After Congress passed the Selective Service Act requiring all men aged 21–30 to register, Goldman and her associates sprang into action to preserve the liberty of Americans. In a personal letter to her friend Agnes Inglis, Goldman admitted she had not only an ideological opposition to conscription but also a personal one: her brother and three nephews all were of draft age. The coercion of objectors particularly raised Goldman's ire; she lumped it together with "the hundred and one other outrageous tyrannies" that war-time America fastened upon its people.[76] Goldman commented in another letter on the hypocrisy of "a democracy like America" denying the considerations of conscientious objectors.[77] She contended that as a woman not subject to military service, she could not advise people on the matter, but she could plead the case of those who refused to be coerced into military service and stand by their actions. Goldman and her comrades did not expect they could "stem the tidal wave of hatred and violence" that conscription would bring, but they felt they must at least raise awareness that many in the United States "owned their souls" and "meant to preserve their integrity."[78] Thus, they called a conference in the *Mother Earth* office on May 9 to organize the No-Conscription League and make plans. The group wrote a manifesto and organized a series of mass meetings in New York City. Goldman assumed the group would face resistance from the government and "patriotic jingoes," as similar organizations faced in Europe, but she promised to go forward and "spare no effort to make the voice of protest a moral force in the life of this country."[79] Through "some propaganda," Goldman hoped she and her cohort could "call attention to the autocracy contained in conscription."[80]

A mass mailing of the manifesto went out near the end of May. A drawing of a bare-chested man facing the barrel of a cannon with a torn "conscription" banner in his hands adorned the front of the two-page pamphlet. The manifesto noted that England was engaged in war for eighteen months before imposing compulsory military service, but "free America" passed a conscription bill mere weeks after declaring war.[81] Furthermore, European nations recognized the rights of conscientious objectors, but "this democratic country makes no such provision for those who will not commit murder at the behest of the profiteers through human sacrifice." Thus, "the 'land of the free and the home of the brave' is ready to coerce free men into the military yoke."[82] The pamphlet outlined the league's platform of protest:

> We oppose conscription because we are internationalists, antimilitarists, and opposed to all wars waged by capitalist governments. We will fight for what we choose to fight for; we will never fight simply because we are ordered to fight. We believe that the militarization of America is an evil that far outweighs, in its antisocial and antilibertarian effects, any good that may come from America's participation in the war. We will resist conscription by every means in our power, and we will sustain those who, for similar reasons, refuse to be conscripted.[83]

A June 1917 *Mother Earth* article copied much of the manifesto verbatim and encouraged readers to write in for the full pamphlet to distribute.[84] Unlike the article, however, the pamphlet indicted the press and pulpit as co-conspirators in the ruling class's efforts to "throw sand in the eyes of the masses and to blind them to the real issue confronting them." Furthermore, the manifesto predicted that freedom of speech, assembly, and the press would be "thrown upon the dungheap of political guarantees" along with the ability of men to choose whether to participate in war. The pamphlet concluded with a plea to organize meetings and send money for the cause, which would help the league publish additional literature against militarism and conscription.[85]

Newspapers across the country took note of the pamphlet, emphasizing that it emanated from the *Mother Earth* office. Articles labeled the manifesto as "insidious and dangerous" propaganda urging Americans to "disregard and disobey the law."[86] Some noted that the pamphlet had been carefully worded to avoid mentioning registration, but the circular had gained authorities' attention, and the league's members were being monitored.[87] According to the New York *Sun*, a personal letter from

Goldman accompanied the pamphlet, begging for funds to campaign against conscription via meetings, manifestos, and *Mother Earth.*[88] By the time *Mother Earth* published its June issue, Goldman boasted that the league had circulated 100,000 copies of its initial manifesto.[89]

Mother Earth Laments Democracy's Death

Goldman devoted the entire June 1917 *Mother Earth* to essays on conscription. The issue's cover bore a thick black frame around the words "June 5th/In Memoriam: American Democracy"—June 5 being Registration Day. In addition to the condensed manifesto with Goldman's commentary, Goldman wrote and carefully selected essays for the issue that exemplified the No-Conscription League's stance on war and compulsory service.

Essays by Goldman and her nephew Saxe Commins referred to Moloch, a fiery deity to whom the men of Judah sacrificed their children. As "the monster" of "Moloch Militarism" reached out for the youth of the land, both he and the god of wealth Mammon would be made immortal.[90] Via conscription, Reitman argued in his contribution, America had entered the "business of wholesale slaughter."[91] Themes of murder and devastation carried throughout the issue. W. S. Van Valkenburgh indicated that the public used to meet such widespread loss of life with gasps of horror, but the people had grown callous.[92] In fact, Goldman and Commins lamented that Americans celebrated sending their youth to their deaths with music to "drown out the groans and curses of the unwilling" and colors to "obscure the burning eye of hate."[93] Goldman cited negro lynching to illustrate that in America, "human tragedy ever has been a cause for rejoicing."[94]

Contributors emphasized the loss of liberty associated with conscription. Rather than the democracy America promised, the government had been given unbridled power, and the people now would be subject to a despotic military government.[95] Americans had been stripped not only of their freedom to choose whether to fight but also of their freedom of speech. Van Valkenburgh declared "one dare say nothing, do nothing and think nothing, unless it conforms to the hysteria of the times."[96] Conscientious objectors had fewer rights than anyone, contributors wrote. Reitman averred that America would severely punish citizens who refused to be conscripted. "In war times, not only is your enemy dangerous, but every citizen who refuses to obey orders," he argued.

> America fears Germany much less than she does men and women who refuse to murder for her benefit, and she will be a great deal kinder in her dealings with the external enemy than she may be with her conscientious objectors.[97]

The people accepted war and conscription because they'd been gulled, contributors wrote. Van Valkenburgh fingered the mainstream American press as a co-conspirator "working up the patriotic passions of the people."[98] Randolph Bourne accused the nation's college professors and writers of throwing in with the government to help sway the "[s]luggish masses, too remote from the world conflict to be stirred, too lacking in intellect to perceive their danger!" He argued that intellectuals had guided the nation "through sheer force of ideas into what the other nations entered only through predatory craft or popular hysteria or militarist madness!"[99] Bourne and Reitman declared that America's brightest should hold firm to their ideals and turn their energy toward promoting peace instead of war.[100]

In fact, contributors encouraged the public at large to resist the government. Reitman offered the many European conscientious objectors who had remained resolute under penalty of death as an example, insisting that the only way to end war was to mimic the Russian soldiers who put down their arms and refused to fight. If the government killed the objectors, then at least they died for something they believed in, Reitman averred.[101] Maxwell Bodenheim found hope in the apathy demonstrated at army recruiting stations. He noted that military officers attempted to elicit volunteers via excessive demonstrations of patriotism and speeches spewing half-truths about the war, leading the public to believe the enemy posed an immediate danger to all Americans. As a final plea, recruiters insisted that no one would consider men forced to join through conscription heroic—the only way to demonstrate true patriotism was to volunteer for service before conscription took effect. Yet over the course of several repeat performances, Bodenheim wrote, very few came forward. This, he insisted, was evidence that most Americans "didn't care to enter the war."[102] Commins hoped that the truths delivered in *Mother Earth* would persuade Americans to act per their consciences on Registration Day.[103]

Goldman offered the No-Conscription League meetings as a public way for citizens to make their feelings on war and conscription known. Her article on the league indicated that 8,000 had attended the group's inaugural gathering, and she expected more on the eve of Registration Day.[104] A full-page ad on the back cover of the magazine gave details on the June 4 meeting, calling on "Mothers, Fathers, Sons" to "turn out in protest against conscription!"[105]

New Yorkers Rally Against Conscription

Before Goldman's arrest, the No-Conscription League conducted mass meetings at various locations around New York City. The initial meeting at Harlem River Casino May 18—the day Wilson signed the Selective

Figure 3.4 Free Speech League President Leonard Abbott, a *Mother Earth* contributor and speaker at No-Conscription League meetings, addresses mourners at a New York memorial for anarchists killed in a 1914 bombing.

Source: Library of Congress.

Service Act—served as an introduction to the No-Conscription League. Free Speech League President Leonard Abbott presided; attorney Harry Weinberger was among the platform party.[106] Goldman noted that after the first meeting, advice seekers besieged the *Mother Earth* office, including "frightened youths, fearfully wrought up and at sea as to what to do" and "mothers, imploring us to save their boys." Visitors, phone calls, and letters came by the hundreds as the No-Conscription League prepared for its second rally.[107] On June 4, the eve of Registration Day, the league hosted a protest at Hunt's Point Place in the Bronx.[108]

Both meetings attracted massive crowds of conscription opponents and supporters. Goldman described the scene as she and Berkman approached Hunt's Point Place: "Before us was a human dam, as far as the eye could see, a densely packed, swaying mass, counting tens of thousands." She noted police and soldiers on the outskirts of the mass, "shouting orders, swearing, and pushing the crowd from the sidewalks to the street and back again."[109] Newspaper articles bearing headlines such as

"Emma Goldman Is Bitter Toward Draft" stated that the masses packed the May 18 venue "in utter disregard for fire laws" while police looked on to preserve order.[110] Papers across the country reported riots following the June 4 meeting, where Goldman and Berkman allegedly aroused scores of nonconscriptionists "to the point of frenzy" while thousands of others tried to push their way into the hall from the streets. The papers offered salacious anecdotes of crazed women biting and scratching soldiers while children fell under the mob's feet.[111] Goldman later wrote that the riot "was of editorial making and seemed a deliberate attempt to stop further protests." Nonetheless, police banned further meetings, and the league struggled to find a venue for their next assembly, settling for a small room belonging to the Jewish Socialist Party.[112]

A writer for the New York *Sun* surmised that Goldman incited violence for publicity and to drive the sales of *Mother Earth.*[113] However, Goldman and her colleagues made every attempt to prevent violent outbursts at their meetings. They encouraged attendees of each gathering to control themselves and ignore anyone who tried to make trouble, in the name of peace and freedom. They indicated soldiers who favored conscription had come to disrupt the meeting but that the anarchists would be civil and give no one reason to believe the conscription protests were violent.[114] Goldman later described the "newly-rigged out soldiers" as a "very boisterous lot" who were noisy through all the speakers, even throwing objects at the platform. When Goldman took the stage, "pandemonium broke loose" as the "future heroes…jeered and hooted, intoned the Star-Spangled Banner, and frantically waved small American flags."[115] Newspaper articles indicated that the speakers Goldman scheduled radiated "a revolutionary spirit" while soldiers in uniform were denied the right to offer counterpoints, but Goldman insisted she permitted both sides to voice their opinions in the name of free speech.[116]

Speeches delivered at the New York rallies echoed many of the themes that emerged in the No-Conscription League manifesto and in *Mother Earth* writings on war and conscription, especially the ideas that American democracy and liberty were lies, that the war was for profit, and that militarism spelled death. Goldman and Abbott lamented the "carnal brutality of man, blood-shed and conquest" that militarism brought about. They called the present war one for military power and money, and they insisted that it was only the beginning. Abbott predicted the war would "bring the military monster into our homes, and as it grows stronger it will become more greedy, and the love for conquest will take possession of it, and the next thing that we will be required to do will be to conquer Mexico."[117]

Several speakers grieved for innocent men, women, and children slaughtered abroad as well as for the young American soldiers to be sacrificed at the altar of militarism. Goldman compared America to

Russia, where she had witnessed compulsory military registration as a child—an experience that left a lasting effect on her. "The mothers and the fathers of the whole community turned out in mourning and considered it a day of sorrow and of tears and of pain when their sons were taken away into the Army," she said.[118] Goldman and Abbott argued that the future belonged to the young men, who should be allowed to stay home and become productive members of society rather than being sent to slaughter.[119] Two women at the June 4 gathering implored fellow mothers not to send their sons to war. One, whom Abbott introduced as "Mother Yuster," said that women bring up their sons to make the world better, not worse; they did not bring them up to be "murderers and slaughterers of their fellow men."[120] Similarly, a woman introduced as Mrs. Ballantine could not imagine raising her young son only for him to be sent to war without his consent. She used the occasion to promote birth control, imploring other women not to breed. She begged, "Don't have any more children if that is what you are bringing them up for."[121]

Ever the advocates for the working class, Goldman, Berkman, and Abbott all proclaimed that Americans would prefer to fight the capitalist class at home than some vague enemy abroad. "Neither the soldiers of this country nor the workers have any enemies across the ocean," Berkman declared. "They have an enemy right here in this country...that makes money, millions and billions of it, out of your blood, out of small children and widows, by putting them in sweat shops, by working them all hours."[122] Abbott set up a dichotomy between the nation's "exploiters, capitalists, and militarists" and the "persecuted labor bodies," calling the former the enemy and pledging "deathless loyalty" to the latter.[123] Goldman concurred, avowing that when anarchists proclaimed to love America, they didn't mean Wall Street, John D. Rockefeller, J. P. Morgan, or munitions manufacturers; they meant "America of great pioneers of liberty." She proclaimed that the American people would not fight for the capitalists, who lied about the war being one of freedom. "You have no right to tell the people to give their lives in behalf of democracy, when democracy is the laughing stock before all of Europe," Goldman averred.[124]

America's entry into the war and the subsequent Conscription Bill demonstrated that democracy was a sham, according to Goldman and others who spoke at the meetings. Goldman insisted that the number of people who flocked to No-Conscription League rallies provided evidence of America's overwhelming opposition to the war.[125] The people never were asked if they wanted a war, Goldman asserted. In fact, American voters placed Wilson in office under the pretense that he would keep the United States out of war. "If war is necessary, only the people must decide whether they want war or not," Goldman avowed, "and as long as the people have not given their consent, I deny that the President of the United States has any right to declare it."[126] Furthermore, Goldman insisted that the people had no say through their representatives because the ruling class pulled Congress's strings. She surmised that "each Congressman and each Senator is taken into a private room where spiritualistic mediums are being used, and they are mesmerized and massaged" until they are willing to do as the administration tells them.[127] Peter Kane Jr., a speaker at the June 4 rally, agreed that the people's representatives did not represent them. "We therefore repudiate a declaration of war until the American people, the masses, the workers who do the fighting and pay the taxes for a war are given the right that true democracy guarantees, the right to decide by a referendum whether or not they want war," Kane decreed.[128]

Goldman and her colleagues proclaimed that if the people wanted war, they would volunteer to fight it willingly; the Conscription Bill would be unnecessary. Goldman wondered, "If the people want war, why so much police, why so many soldiers to compel them to become soldiers?" She added conscription would teach the American people that "American Liberty has been buried and is dead and is a corpse." At the same meeting, Berkman similarly declared, "Conscription in a free country means the cemetery of liberty, and if conscription is the cemetery then registration is the undertaker."[129] Berkman and Abbott equated conscription with slavery. "There is a provision in our Constitution forbidding involuntary service," Abbott said. "If conscription does not mean involuntary servitude, then I don't know the meaning of those words." Berkman lamented that the nation had made a holiday of Registration Day, as if it were something to be celebrated. "But something that means your further enslavement," he declared, "something that means the coercion of you to do things against your conscience, against your nature, against the dictates of everything that is fine in you—things like that should be mourned and wept over."[130] Kane promised he would not allow any law to coerce him into murder; he believed that such a law was "tyrannical and fit for autocracies only."[131]

Conscription was but one symptom of the authoritarian government the United States had become. Speakers railed specifically against Kultur—a German brand of authoritarianism that incorporated militarism and racism, which they avowed the American government was adopting. Goldman argued that if the framers of the Declaration of Independence "could look down upon the country and see what their offspring has done to it, how they have outraged it, how they have robbed it, how they have polluted it—why, my friends, they would turn in their graves."[132] A New York school headmaster named Robert Hutchinson, speaking at the June 4 meeting, encouraged Americans start the fight against Kultur on domestic soil, not abroad. "Let us stir up the people to fight for the real freedom that democracy means," he proclaimed. "Let us stir them up to fight for more than the mere word; let us stir them up to fight so that freedom and democracy be made facts." Berkman concurred, avowing that those who seemed "so generous with liberty as to carry it to Germany across the sea" should fight to "retain liberty right here in our country."[133]

Freedom of speech was paramount among the liberties for which Goldman and her colleagues advocated. Abbott surmised a country "must have a guilty conscience" when it arrests young men and women "on flimsy charges" for speaking their mind, breaks up meetings without pretext, and suppresses publications. Berkman believed all speech should be tolerated: anarchists and their opponents. Furthermore, he contended that any soldier who claimed to be a patriot should fight for everyone's freedoms, not just those with like minds. He urged the enlisted men to "consider whether you have the right to suppress those who do not believe as you do. Consider well, especially if you pretend to fight under the banner of free speech and liberty."[134] Goldman and Abbott promised that despite attempts at suppression, they and other anarchists would remain steadfast. "Anarchists show their convictions in war times as well as times of peace," Abbott declared.[135] Goldman denied that so-called patriots, police, or gentlemen with wealth or power could stop the revolutionary spirit. She repeatedly expressed willingness to take any consequences for her words—whether it be prison or death—if it meant standing up for her ideals. She proclaimed, "I would rather die the death of a lion than live the life of a dog." Furthermore, Goldman promised that for every idealist imprisoned or shot, thousands would rise in their place. Eventually, she predicted, the voices would be

> raised into a thunder, and people of America will rise and say, we want to be a democracy, to be sure, but we want the kind of democracy which means liberty and opportunity to every man and woman in America.[136]

Speakers at the June 4 meeting frequently mentioned the liberty Morris Becker and Louis Kramer deserved, and the No-Conscription League organized a June 14 rally on their behalf.[137] Police arrested Becker and Kramer, as well as Joseph Walker and Louis Sternberg, for passing out handbills advertising the Hunt's Point Place rally outside a peace meeting at Madison Square Garden on June 1. Federal Judge Julius Mayer acquitted Walker and Sternberg but convicted Becker and Kramer of conspiracy to advise against registering; Kramer received an extended sentence for refusing to register himself. Much like the headlines after Czolgosz assassinated McKinley, national news coverage of the arrests emphasized Goldman's influence on the men, even calling them her "disciples."[138] Goldman later wrote that the No-Conscription League did not need to do much to publicize their June 14 protest of the arrests, other than call the newspapers. According to Goldman, the press "denounced our impudence in continuing anti-war activities, and they sharply criticized the authorities for failing to stop us."[139]

Perhaps the police were reading the newspapers; they used the June 14 mass meeting as a trap to round up dozens of men who had failed to register. In a lengthy article, the *Sun* reported that 30,000 people gathered to watch "the operation of a Federal mousetrap for slackers and anarchists." Hundreds of policemen and soldiers stood ready "to smash a riot if one should develop."[140] Authorities allowed the meeting to occur but recorded Berkman and Goldman's tirades against President Wilson and Judge Mayer.[141] Then, as the attendees who had filled the hall "to suffocation" attempted to leave, policemen and deputy marshals blocked the exits. They asked each man for his registration card, which all but thirty-five of the 400 men present were able to produce. Marshals questioned the thirty-five men without cards but jailed only two; the *New York Times* identified one of the arrested as an immigrant who "had no use for the United States."[142] The No-Conscription League had planned another rally for June 23, but after the trap, Goldman decided she would have no more meetings unless she could be sure those who had not registered would keep away; she would concentrate her No-Conscription League activities on the printed word.[143]

Patriotic Press Attacks Anarchists

The newspapers disagreed with Goldman and her colleagues about Americans' beliefs and wants. Articles about No-Conscription League activities were steeped in language of "otherness," drawing a sharp distinction between "us"—true American patriots—and "them"—anarchists who were largely foreign immigrants intent on importing foreign values. For instance, newspaper coverage of the May 18 meeting emphasized the distribution of propaganda at the door imploring American workers to follow Russia's lead and form a committee against the war.[144] Furthermore, accounts of the meetings noted the number of foreign-born in the audience.[145] Coverage of Goldman's followers' arrests also noted their foreign-ness and specifically their lack of U.S. citizenship.[146] Some meeting recaps singled out shouts from conscription supporters telling the speakers to "go back to Russia."[147] Editorials echoed that sentiment, noting that Goldman's "breed of cattle is not indigenous to American soil." Some editorials labeled her a "red" and declared if she could not respect the privilege of living in the United States or side with the nation in its time of crisis, she should be deported.[148]

Figure 3.5 A Registration Day cartoon in the *Chicago Tribune* differentiated between men who dutifully registered and "slackers" who evaded the draft.

Articles on Goldman's anti-conscription activities were mere drops in an ocean of conscription coverage that further enhanced the us and them dichotomy. During the few weeks that the No-Conscription League operated, newspaper pages teemed with articles covering every angle of the draft, overwhelmingly showing support for the conscription measure and deeming it patriotic. For example, the Registration Day issue of the *Chicago Daily Tribune* carried a bold banner across the top of the front page that read, "**ENROLLING LIBERTY ARMY/** PATRIOTS WILL REGISTER GLADLY—ALL OTHERS MUST." The page also featured a cartoon split in two frames, with Uncle Sam stamping "Registered Male" on the backs of smiling men in suits and skimmer hats in one frame and chastising a group of sullen, hatless "Registration Dodgers" in the other.[149] In addition to stories on the draft itself, articles explaining why the United States fought flanked the cartoon, including one that declared young men should rejoice at the opportunity to enter combat for the fundamentals of liberty.[150]

Because of this widespread patriotism, newspaper articles expressed the belief that speech against the government during wartime was treason. Articles labeled Goldman and her colleagues as traitors and indicated they should be treated as such. Several editorials indicated that Goldman's tirades may have been tolerated previously, but as one editorial eloquently put it, "monkeying with Uncle Sam in peace is a different proposition from pestering the old gentleman with a war on his hands."[151] The newspapers averred that free speech had limits, and Goldman had exceeded them in her attempts to hamper the war effort.[152]

Many prophetically suggested that to silence her, authorities should imprison her until the end of the war.[153] According to some editorials, jailing Goldman would serve as a good example to others who may seek to test the bounds of free speech.[154] A few bold editors suggested that jailing was not enough; Goldman and her ilk should pay for their treasonous speech with their lives.[155] As Goldman's meetings and mailings continued, newspapers questioned why the authorities allowed her to persist, especially when government censors targeted loyal American newspapers that voluntarily kept their columns in check.[156] Some editorials pointed out the government's fear that arresting Goldman would make her a martyr, but at least one urged the government to let her be a martyr; arresting her would do more good than harm.[157]

Goldman thanked the newspapers for their coverage, particularly the press of New York, for rendering her anti-conscription work more service "than a thousand Emma Goldmans could render." In her June 4 speech, she acknowledged that the "blood curdling articles" were not intended to publicize her cause but to paralyze supporters into silence, making them believe they would be imprisoned or shot on the spot for attending No-Conscription League meetings. The press, she proclaimed, advocated for America to hang and quarter her and other anarchists. Nonetheless, Goldman believed the press coverage had enlarged and emboldened her audience. "They don't know, the poor chaps, that if anyone has an ideal, you can't terrorize him no matter what you do," Goldman declared. "So I am personally grateful to you—to the press."[158]

Mother Earth Raid and Arrest

On June 15, 1917, the newspapers got their wish for Goldman's arrest. Federal authorities arrested Goldman and Berkman in their 125th Street offices in New York late in the afternoon. Their arrests occurred on the same day, quite appropriately, that President Wilson signed the controversial Espionage Act into law.[159] The act included provisions to limit expression that "intended to incite, provoke and encourage resistance to the United States in war."[160] With the ink still fresh on the new law, Goldman and Berkman were instead charged with "conspiracy to induce persons not to register" for the draft under the Selective Service Act, which Wilson signed nearly a month earlier.[161]

When federal authorities raided Goldman's offices, they were interested in more than arresting two of the nation's most infamous radicals; they were also searching for information regarding *Mother Earth*'s subscribers and who attended the recent anti-conscription meetings.[162] Harry Weinberger—who worked closely with the Free Speech League protecting speakers such as Sanger, labor activists, and other radicals of the era—immediately joined Goldman and Berkman in their case.[163] Two years later, Weinberger stood before the Supreme Court to defend anarchist Jacob Abrams against charges for violating the Espionage Act in one of the turning-point cases for how justices interpreted the First Amendment. After Goldman and Berkman were arrested, Weinberger fought and ultimately secured his clients' release on bail just days before their trial in federal court.[164] The next chapter examines the trial as well as how the mainstream press grappled with the issues it raised.

Notes

1 Claire Goldstene, *The Struggle for America's Promise: Equal Opportunity at the Dawn of Corporate Capital* (Jackson: University Press of Mississippi, 2014), 69–71, 81; Vivian Gornick, *Emma Goldman: Revolution as a Way of Life* (New Haven, CT: Yale University Press, 2011), 17; Ann Massa, "Chicago's Martyrs: A Parable for the People," *Chicago History* 15, 2 (1986): 54–63.

2 Emma Goldman, *Living My Life* (Garden City, NY: Garden City Publishing, 1934), 10.

3 See "Emma Goldman Buried Near Haymarket Rioters," *Indianapolis Star*, May 18, 1940, and "Emma Goldman Buried: Anarchist Interred Beside Hanged Chicago Rioters," *Gazette* (Montreal, Can.), May 18, 1940.

4 Goldman, *Living My Life*, 3.

5 Goldstene, *Struggle for America's Promise*, 75; Theresa Moritz and Albert Moritz, *The World's Most Dangerous Woman: A New Biography of Emma Goldman* (Vancouver: Subway Books, 2002), 8; Alice Wexler, *Emma Goldman: An Intimate Life* (New York: Pantheon Books, 1984), 40–45, 51–54, 167–168.

6 Bonnie Haaland, *Emma Goldman: Sexuality and the Impurity of the State* (New York: Black Rose Books, 1993), xi; Wexler, *Intimate Life*, 54, 57–58.
7 Kenneth C. Wenzer, *Anarchists Adrift: Emma Goldman and Alexander Berkman* (St. James, NY: Brandywine Press, 1996).
8 Haaland, *Sexuality and Impurity of the State*, xi; Wexler, *Intimate Life*, 83–85, 88–89.
9 Keith Cassidy, "The American Left and the Problem of Leadership, 1900–1920," *South Atlantic Quarterly* 82, 4 (1983), 387–388; Goldstene, *Struggle for America's Promise*, 73–74; Wexler, *Intimate Life*, 91–94.
10 Goldstene, *Struggle for America's Promise*, 75–76; Wenzer, *Anarchists Adrift*, 35–36; Wexler, *Intimate Life*, 62–65.
11 Goldman, *Living My Life*, 87–95.
12 Goldman, *Living My Life,* 99–101. For examples of the newspaper coverage, see "Anarchists in Hiding," *New York Tribune*, June 25, 1892; "Full of Grit," *Boston Globe*, June 25, 1892; "Proof of a Plot Now Produced," *Pittsburgh Dispatch*, June 25, 1892.
13 "Anarchy's Den," *New York World*, July 28, 1892.
14 Wenzer, *Anarchists Adrift*, 36.
15 Goldstene, *Struggle for America's Promise*, 76–78; Gornick, *Revolution as a Way of Life*, 37.
16 Goldman, *Living My Life*, 123; "Almost Fizzled," *St. Louis Post-Dispatch*, August 20, 1893.
17 See, for example, "Anarchists Kept in Check," *New York Times*, August 20, 1893; "Emma Would Speak," *Chicago Tribune*, August 20, 1893; "Emma Talks," *Brooklyn Daily Eagle*, August 20, 1893.
18 Goldman, *Living My Life*, 129–130. For an excerpt of the trial transcript, see *The People v. Emma Goldman*, in Candice Falk, *Emma Goldman: A Documentary History of the American Years*, Vol. 1 (Berkley: University of California Press, 2003), 161–176. For examples of trial coverage, see "Emma's Trial Begun," *New York World*, October 4, 1893; "Trial of Emma Goldman," *New York Tribune*, October 5, 1893; "Emma Goldman on Trial," *New York Times,* October 5, 1893.
19 *The People v. Emma Goldman*, 176.
20 Goldman, *Living My Life*, 130–148.
21 Don Sneed, "Newspapers Call for Swift Justice: A Study of the McKinley Assassination," *Journalism Quarterly* 65, 2 (Summer 1988): 360–398.
22 Goldman, *Living My Life*, 296–297. See "President McKinley Shot by an Assassin," *Courier-Journal* (Louisville, KY), September 7, 1901; "McKinley's Life in the Balance," *Boston Globe*, September 7, 1901; "Assassin Confesses," *Nashville American*, September 7, 1901.
23 Goldman, *Living My Life*, 299–310.
24 *Washington Post*, September 11, 1901, quoted in Sneed, "Newspapers Call for Swift Justice," 364.
25 Emma Goldman, "The Tragedy at Buffalo," *Free Society*, October 6, 1901, republished in *Mother Earth*, October 1906, 11–16; Goldman, *Living My Life*, 312.
26 See Max Baginski, "Leon Czolgosz," *Mother Earth*, October 1906, 4–9; Emma Goldman, "The Tragedy at Buffalo" (reprint of her 1901 *Free Society* essay), *Mother Earth*, October 1906, 11–16.

27 Gornick, *Revolution as a Way of Life*, 39–40; Wenzer, *Anarchists Adrift*, 41.
28 Wenzer, *Anarchists Adrift*, 41–42; Wexler, *Intimate Life*, 79, 116–118, 188–194, 201–207.
29 Peter Glassgold, *Anarchy! An Anthology of Emma Goldman's* Mother Earth (Berkeley, CA: Counterpoint, 2012), xxviii; Goldstene, *Struggle for America's Promise*, 78; Haaland, *Sexuality and Impurity in the State*, xii; Wexler, *Intimate Life*, 139–161, 165–175. For more on Goldman and Reitman's relationship, see Falk, *Love, Anarchy, and Emma Goldman*, and Suzanne Poirier, "Emma Goldman, Ben Reitman, and Reitman's Wives: A Study in Relationships," *Women's Studies* 14, 3 (1988): 277–297.
30 Wexler, *Intimate Life*, 121. See also Haaland, *Sexuality and Impurity in the State*, xii.
31 Glassgold, *Anarchy!*; Wexler, *Intimate Life*, 121–130.
32 Linda Lumsden, "Anarchy Meets Feminism: A Gender Analysis of Emma Goldman's *Mother Earth*, 1906–1917," *American Journalism* 24, 3 (2007): 31–54; Wexler, *Intimate Life*, 193–199.
33 Goldman, *Living My Life*, 377–378.
34 Ibid., 378.
35 Emma Goldman and Max Baginski, "Mother Earth," *Mother Earth*, March 1906, 1–4.
36 Glassgold, *Anarchy!*, xviii.
37 See "Woman Anarchist Calls Our Flag a Sham," *New York Times*, April 2, 1906.
38 See "Berkman in Detroit, Meets Emma Goldman," *New York Times*, May 20, 1906; "Hailed as New Chief by Reds," *Pittsburgh Press*, May 20, 1906; "Emma Goldman Chief of Anarchists Since the Death of Johann Most," *Democrat and Chronicle* (Rochester, NY), May 21, 1906, "An Anarchistic Romance," *News and Observer* (Raleigh, NC), May 23, 1906.
39 Glassgold, *Anarchy!*, xxiv–xxv; Bill Lynskey, "'I Shall Speak in Philadelphia': Emma Goldman and the Free Speech League," *Pennsylvania Magazine of History & Biography* 133, 2 (2009): 167; Rebecca Parker, "An Analysis of Emma Goldman's Free Speech Campaign Strategies" (master's thesis, Western Illinois University, 1971), 32–38.
40 Police broke up an October 1906 meeting to protest the arrest of three speakers at a previous anarchist assembly; Goldman was among six women and three men who were arrested. Emma Goldman, "Police Brutality," *Mother Earth*, November 1906, 2–3.
41 Lynskey, "I Shall Speak in Philadelphia"; Parker, "An Analysis of Emma Goldman's Free Speech Campaigns"; Wexler, *Intimate Life*, 176–182.
42 David M. Rabban, *Free Speech in the Forgotten Years* (Cambridge: Cambridge University Press, 1997), 76. See also David Brudnoy, "Theodore Schroeder and the Suppressers of Vice," *Civil Liberties Review* 3, 2 (1976): 48–56; Lynskey, "I Shall Speak in Philadelphia," 140.
43 Goldman, *Living My Life*, 346–347.
44 *Turner v. Williams*, 194 U.S. 279, 283, 292 (1904); Goldman, *Living My Life*, 347–348. See also Emma Goldman to Abe Isaak, December 4, 1903, and Emma Goldman, "For Freedom," *Cronaca Sovversiva,* November 29, 1903 (trans. from Italian), both in Falk, *Emma Goldman*, Vol. 2 (2005), 121–125.

45 Goldman, *Living My Life*, 456–459; Voltairine de Cleyre, "The Free Speech Fight in Philadelphia," *Mother Earth*, October 1909, 237–239; "In Defense of Free Speech," *Mother Earth*, October 1909, 241–248; Lynskey, "I Shall Speak in Philadelphia."

46 Voltairine de Cleyre had delivered the address at a New York rally supporting Goldman in her dispute with Philadelphia officials; "Our Police Censorship," *Mother Earth*, November 1909, 300–301.

47 The pamphlet also included newspaper articles, essays, and legal opinion by Free Speech League attorney Theodore Schroeder; see "The Fight for Free Speech" (East Orange, NJ, 1909).

48 Weda C. Addicks, "Protest of Mrs. Addicks: The Prominent Mayflower Descendant," *Philadelphia Public Ledger*, reprinted in "The Fight for Free Speech."

49 Articles from the *Providence Bulletin*, *Chicago Record-Herald*, and *Hartford Courant* all appear under the heading "Consummate Asses," *Burlington* (VT) *Daily News*, October 7, 1909.

50 "Denial of Free Speech," *Harrisburg* (PA) *Daily Independent*, October 18, 1909.

51 Goldman, *Living My Life*, 185–187.

52 Ibid., 552–553, 569.

53 Wexler, *An Intimate Life*, 210–211.

54 Harry Breckenridge, "The Persecution of Margaret Sanger," *Mother Earth*, November 1914, 296–297; "The Sanger Case," *Mother Earth*, January 1915, 380.

55 "The Sanger Case," 379–380.

56 Craig L. LaMay, "America's Censor: Anthony Comstock and Free Speech," *Communications & The Law* 19, 3 (September 1997).

57 Act of March 3, 1873, ch. 258, § 2, 17 *Stat* 599.

58 Emma Goldman and Max Baginski, "Mother Earth," *Mother Earth*, March 1906, 3; John R. Corvell, "Comstockery," *Mother Earth*, March 1906, 30–40.

59 *Mother Earth*, April 1906, 16.

60 Alexander Berkman, "Comstock and Mother Earth," *Mother Earth*, February 1910, 369–370.

61 Emma Goldman, "My dear sir" (to the press), February 1916, in Candace Falk, with Ronald J. Zboray, et al., eds., *The Emma Goldman Papers: A Microfilm Edition* (Alexandria, VA: Chadwyck-Healey, Inc., 1990; hereafter referred to as Goldman Papers), reel 9. The letter is undated but would have been written between the date of her arrest and the March 1 protest.

62 Emma Goldman to W. S. Van Valkenburgh, February 21, 1916, Goldman Papers, reel 9.

63 "Emma Goldman Dares Police to Still Her," *Sun* (New York), March 2, 1916. See also "Emma Goldman to Women," *New York Times*, March 2, 1916.

64 Emma Goldman, "The Social Aspects of Birth Control," *Mother Earth*, April 1916, 475. See also Emma Goldman, "An Urgent Appeal to My Friends," *Mother Earth*, April 1916, 450–451.

65 Goldman, *Living My Life*, 570–572; Emma Goldman, "The Petty Discrimination of the Law," *Mother Earth*, December 1916, 702.

66 Emma Goldman, "My Arrest and Preliminary Hearing," *Mother Earth*, March 1916, 430.

67 Goldman, *Living My Life*, 572.

68 Alexander Berkman, "In Reply to Kropotkin," *Mother Earth*, November 1914, 280–282. See also Guy de Maupassant, "War: The Triumph of Barbarism," *Mother Earth*, August 1914, 213–216; "If We Must Fight, Let Us Fight for the Social Revolution," *Mother Earth*, October 1914, 255–260.

69 Goldman and Berkman were among more than thirty anarchists who signed the manifesto, to be issued not only via the press but also in pamphlets. "International Anarchist Manifesto on the War," *Mother Earth*, May 1915, in Glassgold, *Anarchy!*, 385–388.

70 Don, "The Fallacies of War," *Mother Earth*, February 1917, 770.

71 "Two Attitudes," *Freedom* (London), October 1915, reprinted in *Mother Earth*, November 1916, 443–447. See also "Observations and Comments," *Mother Earth*, January 1917, 722–723.

72 A Mother of Seven Children, "Birth Control," *Mother Earth*, April 1916, 478.

73 Goldman, *Living My Life*, 594.

74 Emma Goldman, "The Promoters of the War Mania," *Mother Earth*, March 1917, 5–10. See also Ben Reitman, "Why You Shouldn't Go to War—Refuse to Kill or Be Killed," *Mother Earth*, April 1917, 41–44.

75 Goldman, "Promoters of the War Mania," 8.

76 Emma Goldman to Agnes Inglis, May 3, 1917, Goldman Papers, reel 10.

77 Emma Goldman to Agnes Inglis, May 12, 1917, Goldman Papers, reel 10.

78 Goldman, *Living My Life*, 598.

79 Emma Goldman, "The No-Conscription League," *Mother Earth*, June 1917, 113–114.

80 Goldman to Inglis, May 12, 1917.

81 The United States officially entered the war on April 6, 1917.

82 *No Conscription!* (New York: No-Conscription League, 1917), Goldman Papers, reel 48.

83 Ibid.

84 Goldman, "The No Conscription League," 114.

85 *No Conscription!*

86 "Seize Plot Literature," *Chicago Daily Tribune,* May 30, 1917; "Distinguished as Treason," *Hartford Courant*, June 1, 1917; *New York Tribune*, May 28, 1917; "'Resist Conscription,' Urges League in 100,000 Circulars," *New York Tribune*, May 30, 1917; "New York Threatens Trouble," *Salina* (KS) *Daily Union*, May 30, 1917.

87 "Emma Goldman Defiant," *Evening Public Ledger* (Philadelphia), May 30, 1917; "Declares 10,000 Men Will Ignore Draft," *Washington* (DC) *Herald*, May 31, 1917; "Emma Goldman Lists 5,000 As Against Draft," *Sun* (New York), May 30, 1917; "New York Threatens Trouble"; "Resist Conscription."

88 "Emma Goldman Lists 5,000 As Against Draft."

89 Goldman, "No Conscription League," 113.

90 Emma Goldman, "The Holiday," *Mother Earth*, June 1917, 97; Saxe Commins, "June 5th," *Mother Earth*, June 1917, 105. Regarding the financial motivations of the war, see also Ben Reitman, "Conscription," *Mother Earth*, June 1917, 112; W. S. Van Valkenburgh, "The Turning of the Tide," *Mother Earth*, June 1917, 115; and Randolph Bourne, "The War and the Intellectuals," *Mother Earth*, June 1917, 118.

91 Reitman, "Conscription," 108.

92 Van Valkenburgh, "Turning of the Tide," 114.

93 Goldman, "Holiday"; Commins, "July 5th," 106.

94 Goldman, "Holiday."

95 Commins, "June 5th," 107; Reitman, "Conscription," 108; Van Valkenburgh, "Turning of the Tide," 115.

96 Van Valkenburgh, "Turning of the Tide," 115. See also Commins, "June 5th," 107; Reitman, "Conscription," 110–111.

97 Reitman, "Conscription," 111. See also Van Valkenburgh, "Turning of the Tide," 115.

98 Van Valkenburgh, "Turning of the Tide," 116.

99 Bourne, "War and the Intellectuals," 117.

100 Ibid., 119–122; Reitman, "Conscription," 112.

101 Reitman, "Conscription," 110–112.

102 Maxwell Bodenheim, "Army Recruiting—Methods," *Mother Earth*, June 1917, 122–124.

103 Commins, "June 5th," 107.

104 Goldman, "No-Conscription League," 113.

105 *Mother Earth*, June 1917, back cover.

106 Goldman, *Living My Life*, 599.

107 Ibid., 600.

108 "Seven Indictments," *Los Angeles Times,* June 5, 1917; "Mob Fights Police to Reach Anti-Conscription Meeting," *Democrat and Chronicle* (Rochester, NY), June 5, 1917

109 Goldman, *Living My Life*, 604.

110 "Radicals Urge Resistance to Draft Measures," *New York Tribune*, May 19, 1917; "Emma Goldman Is Bitter Toward Draft," *Albuquerque Journal*, May 19, 1917; "Anarchists Demand Strike to End War," *New York Times*, May 19, 1917.

111 "Anarchists Awed by Police Clubs," *New York Times*, June 5, 1917; "26,000 in Riot in Bronx over Conscription," *Sun* (New York), June 5, 1917; "Antidraft Mob Riots," *Washington Post*, June 5, 1917. Various wire stories carried the news across the country. See, for example, "Soldiers Crack Slacker Heads in Street Row," *Chicago Tribune*, June 5, 1917; "Thousands Seek to Break Police Lines," *Indianapolis News*, June 5, 1917; "Draft Riots Break Out in New York," *Pittsburgh Daily Post*, June 5, 1917; "Riot Against Draft," *Bremen* (IN) *Enquirer*, June 7, 1917.

112 Goldman, *Living My Life*, 607.

113 "Goldman, Berkman & Company," *Sun* (New York), June 6, 1917.

114 Emma Goldman, "We Don't Believe in Conscription" (speech, New York City, May 18, 1917), Goldman Papers, reel 48; "Meeting of

the No-Conscription League" (transcript, New York City, June 4, 1917), Goldman Papers, reel 48; Emma Goldman, "Speech Against Conscription and War" (speech, New York City, June 14, 1917), Goldman Papers, reel 48.

115 Goldman, *Living My Life*, 599–600, 604–606. See also newspaper accounts of soldiers throwing items at the speakers: "Anarchists Awed by Police Clubs," "Soldiers Crack Slacker Heads," "Riot Against Draft."

116 "New Yorkers Applaud While Emma Goldman Denounces Draft Law," *Washington Herald*, May 19, 1917; "Radicals Urge Resistance to Draft Measures"; Goldman, *Living My Life*, 600.

117 "Meeting of the No-Conscription League." See also "We Don't Believe in Conscription."

118 "Meeting of the No-Conscription League."

119 Ibid.; "We Don't Believe in Conscription"; "Speech Against Conscription and War."

120 "Meeting of the No-Conscription League."

121 Ibid.

122 Ibid.

123 Ibid.

124 "We Don't Believe in Conscription."

125 Ibid.; "Meeting of the No-Conscription League"; "Speech Against Conscription and War."

126 "Speech Against Conscription and War."

127 "We Don't Believe in Conscription."

128 Abbott introduced Kane only as a "young man of conscriptable age"; see "Meeting of the No-Conscription League."

129 "Meeting of the No-Conscription League." Goldman made similar arguments in her May 18 speech; see "We Don't Believe in Conscription."

130 "Meeting of the No-Conscription League."

131 Ibid.

132 "Speech Against Conscription and War." See also "We Don't Believe in Conscription."

133 "Meeting of the No-Conscription League."

134 Ibid.

135 Ibid.

136 Ibid.; "We Don't Believe in Conscription"; "Speech Against Conscription and War."

137 "Meeting of the No-Conscription League."

138 Goldman, *Living My Life*, 603; "Two Convicted for Evading the Law," *Durham* (NC) *Morning Herald*, June 13, 1917; "Antidraft Men Guilty," *Manchester* (IA) *Democrat-Radio*, June 13, 1917; "Anarchists Guilty in Anti-Draft Case," *New York Times*, June 13, 1917; "Anarchists Guilty of Anti-Draft Plot," *Sun* (New York), June 13, 1917; "3 Year Term Given Anarchist Slacker," *Sun* (New York), June 14, 1917.

139 Goldman, *Living My Life*, 607.

140 "30,000 Look on at Roundup of 'Reds,'" *Sun* (New York), June 15, 1917. The *New York Times* estimated the crowd at "at least 20,000"; see "Anarchists Assail Mayer," *New York Times*, June 15, 1917.

141 For a transcript of Goldman's speech, see "Speech Against Conscription and War."

142 "Anarchists Assail Mayer"; "30,000 Look on at Roundup of 'Reds'"; Goldman, *Living My Life*, 609.

143 "Speech Against Conscription and War"; Goldman, *Living My Life*, 609.

144 "Radicals Urge Resistance to Draft Measures"; "Anarchists Demand Strike to End War"; "Anarchists Plot Against US Army," *Washington Post*, June 3, 1917; "The Goldman Followers," *Durham* (NC) *Morning Herald*, June 13, 1917.

145 "Anarchists Demand Strike to End War"; "26,000 in Riot in Bronx over Conscription."

146 "Anarchists Guilty of Anti-Draft Plot"; "30,000 Look on at Roundup of 'Reds.'"

147 "Draft Riots Break Out in New York"; "Riot Against Draft"; "26,000 in Riot in Bronx over Conscription."

148 "One Serious Menace," *Courier-News* (Bridgewater, NJ), June 6, 1917; "Treason Unashamed," *Asheville* (NC) *Citizen-Times*, June 3, 1917; "Scores No Conscription League," *Oswego* (KS) *Independent*, June 1, 1917.

149 *Chicago Daily Tribune*, June 5, 1917 (emphasis in original).

150 "A Fateful Day: Rejoice In It, Young Men!", *Chicago Daily Tribune*, June 5, 1917.

151 *Greensboro* (NC) *Daily News*, June 1, 1917.

152 "Preaching Disloyalty," *Washington Post*, May 20, 1917; "Miss Goldman," *Salina* (KS) *Daily Union*, June 2, 1917; *Honolulu Star-Bulletin*, June 16, 1917; "Rounding Up the Slackers," *Evening News* (Wilkes-Barre, PA), June 16, 1917; "The Goldman Followers," *Durham* (NC) *Morning Herald*, June 13, 1917; "Pleading the Baby Act," *Lincoln* (NE) *Star*, June 6, 1917; *Indianapolis Star*, June 6, 1917; "Treason Unashamed," *Asheville* (NC) *Citizen-Times*, June 3, 1917; "First Principles," *Escanaba* (MI) *Morning Press*, June 3, 1917.

153 "Preaching Disloyalty"; "Too Much Freedom," *Durham* (NC) *Morning Herald*, June 1, 1917; *Honolulu Star-Bulletin*, June 16, 1917; "Their Place Is In Jail," *Philadelphia Inquirer*, June 1, 1917; *Democrat and Chronicle* (Rochester, NY), May 23, 1917.

154 "Rounding Up the Slackers"; "Goldman, Berkman & Company."

155 *High Point* (NC) *Enterprise,* June 7, 1917; *Greensboro* (NC) *Daily News*, June 7, 1917.

156 *Argus-Leader* (Sioux Falls, SD), June 1, 1917; *Charlotte News*, June 7, 1917; *Fort Scott* (KS) *Daily Tribune*, June 5, 1917; *Jasper* (MO) *News*, May 27, 1917. For more on wartime censorship of the mainstream press, see Margaret Blanchard, *Revolutionary Sparks: Freedom of Expression in Modern America* (New York: Oxford University Press, 1992), 76–80, and Donald Johnson, "Wilson, Burleson, and Censorship in the First World War," *Journal of Southern History* 28, 1 (1962): 46–58.

157 *Leavenworth* (KS) *Times*, June 16, 1917. See also "Emma Goldman Has Rap at Conscription," *Honolulu Star-Bulletin*, June 15, 1917; "Emma Goldman Allowed to Talk Against Conscription," *Lincoln* (NE) *Star*,

June 15, 1917; "Emma Goldman Talks, Martyrdom Denied Her," *St. Louis Star and Times*, June 15, 1917; *Daily Gazette* (Lawrence, KS), June 16, 1917.

158 "Meeting of the No-Conscription League."

159 Geoffrey R. Stone, "Judge Learned Hand and the Espionage Act of 1917: A Mystery Unraveled," *University of Chicago Law Review* 70, 1 (2003): 336–337.

160 *Abrams v. United States*, 250 U.S. 616, 617 (1919).

161 Richard Drinnon, *Rebel in Paradise: A Biography of Emma Goldman* (Chicago: University of Chicago Press, 2012), 188. See Act of May 18, 1917, ch. 15, 40 *Stat* 76.

162 Goldman, *Living My Life,* 611–612.

163 Richard Polenberg, *Fighting Faiths: The Abrams Case, the Supreme Court, and Free Speech* (Ithaca, NY: Cornell University Press, 1999), 75–81; Rabban, *Free Speech in the Forgotten Years*, 72–73.

164 Goldman, *Living My Life*, 613.

4 Fashioning the Courtroom and Newspapers into Forums for Anarchy

On Emma Goldman's forty-eighth birthday, she and Alexander Berkman were representing themselves in a crowded New York City federal courtroom. Newspapers across the United States celebrated their arrest by publishing headlines such as "Emma Goldman Locked Up," "Noted 'Reds' under Arrest in New York," and "Draft Foes Emma Goldman and Alexander Berkman Seized in Raid."[1] The *New York Times* placed coverage of the pair's capture on the top left corner of its front page on June 16.[2] The lengthy story's jump, placed in the back of the paper, included excerpts from Goldman's and Berkman's acerbic criticisms of the government's new conscription law, which were published in *Mother Earth* and Berkman's publication, *The Blast*. It was these comments, as well as reports of speeches delivered at No-Conscription League rallies, that led to their arrest.[3]

After being placed in police custody, Goldman and Berkman were taken to the Tombs, a New York City detention facility. Goldman's "pugnacious lawyer" Harry Weinberger insisted the two be arraigned and released on bail immediately, but Goldman later wrote that their arrest "had purposely been staged for the late afternoon after the official closing hour" so they would be detained overnight.[4] The next day, she and Berkman appeared in court, where federal attorney Harold Content demanded a high bail for "the leading spirits" in a "country-wide conspiracy to spread anti-conscription propaganda."[5] The U.S. Commissioner who handled the arraignment set bail at $25,000 each; a federal grand jury scheduled the trial to begin on June 27.[6] Goldman, Berkman, and their supporters struggled to secure their bail. Content refused $300,000 worth of real estate offered as bond on what Goldman called "a flimsy technicality," and sufficient cash assets were available to release only one of them. Berkman insisted that Goldman take it. She left the Tombs five days before their trial started and put her full energy over the next three days into raising bail for Berkman. He finally was released on June 25.[7]

With little time to prepare for the trial and even less faith that it would be a fair one, Goldman concluded that she and Berkman should represent themselves and, thus, attempt to turn the trial and its newspaper coverage into forums for disseminating their ideas throughout the nation. Their decision meant parting ways with longtime ally and attorney Weinberger, who rejoined his clients later in the year to help them appeal their convictions. Goldman did not lack faith in Weinberger's abilities. In fact, she wrote to a friend that he was not an ordinary lawyer. "He is above all a man of ideals and of a wonderful fighting spirit, aside of the fact that he is very brilliant," she declared. "I know that if he had gone into court he would have made the fight of his life."[8]

Goldman's decision to forgo counsel represents the first indication of her trial's free expression legacy. Goldman had decided to leverage the trial coverage so she could get her ideas out to a larger audience than she ever could have reached in her speeches in meeting halls throughout the country or through the subscription rolls of *Mother Earth*. Quite ingeniously, Goldman realized that a trial in a federal courtroom might have been, ironically, the only safe forum in 1917 for expressing her ideas to others without government officials stopping her. The court would allow her to speak on her own behalf and to call witnesses that shared her beliefs. While newspaper reporters remained skeptical of her perspectives, they would record and report what was discussed during the trial to a nationwide audience. Goldman later explained, "We would plead our own case, not in order to defend ourselves, but to give public utterance to our ideas." That forum was all she wanted, and she decided she did not need a lawyer for that.[9]

Her approach was likely influenced by her difficulties in circulating the June, anti-conscription-focused, edition of *Mother Earth* to a broader audience weeks earlier. Goldman lamented her organization's limited budget when trying to get the anti-conscription message out. Clearly proud and passionate about the contents of that particular issue, she explained,

> We strained our capital to the last penny to issue an extra large edition. We wanted to mail copies to every Federal officer, to every editor, in our country and to distribute the magazine among young workers and college students.[10]

She settled for circulating 20,000 copies, a number she indicated was not large enough to create the type of impact she sought to make. She took solace, however, in the fact that newspaper reports throughout the nation mentioned *Mother Earth* and her anti-conscription efforts, and they republished parts, small and large, of her anti-conscription manifesto as they covered her arrest by federal authorities. "Fortunately an unexpected ally came to our assistance: the New York newspapers!" Goldman wrote. "The press throughout the country raved at our defiance of law and presidential orders. We duly appreciated their help in making our voices resound through the land."[11] In other words, Goldman came to see the press as a type of unwitting megaphone for her message.

The Associated Press story regarding Goldman's arrest, versions of which appeared in dozens of newspapers, led with her place as editor of *Mother Earth.*[12] The *New York Times, Sun,* and *New York Tribune* all ran front-page articles about her arrest that highlighted her anticonscription ideas.[13] The *New York Times* published 160 words of Goldman's main piece about conscription from the June edition of *Mother Earth,* including Goldman's statement, "The No-Conscription League has been formed for the purpose of encouraging conscientious objectors to affirm their liberty of conscience, and to translate their objection to human slaughter by refusing to participate in the killing of their fellow men."[14] The *Sun* also printed an excerpt of Goldman's writing, as well as some of Berkman's anti-draft ideas from *The Blast.*[15] In each of these instances, Goldman's lament that *Mother Earth* itself did not have the same reach was at least partially assuaged by the presence of her ideas in newspapers.

When it came time for the trial, Goldman was partially successful in fashioning the courtroom into a forum and using the newspaper reporters' notebooks and stories as ways to communicate her ideas throughout the nation. Crucially, the coverage that the trial generated can be divided into two distinct types: daily, news-based trial reports and opinion pieces, such as letters to the editor and editorials that came about as a result of the trial. The wire-service reporters and the staffers for the New York newspapers that covered the trial, in some instances, conveyed the ideas Goldman expressed in the courtroom in their daily reports. Newspaper opinion sections, however, roundly rejected Goldman's ideas, using the trial as an opportunity to publish constructive discussions regarding freedom of expression as well as the types of much less constructive quips that might be found on Twitter in the twenty-first century. In one such example, the *Tulsa Daily World*'s opinion section responded to a question about Goldman's age. While the staff was not certain how old she was, they guessed she was more than forty because a woman "couldn't get that ugly in 40 years."[16] Thus, while Goldman succeeded in encouraging more discourse about her beliefs and freedom of expression within the nation's newspapers, much of it was framed in negative and, at times, non-constructive ways. The trial, for better or worse, led to a dialogue via print media about Goldman's ideas. This chapter explores the perspectives that Goldman and Berkman expressed in the trial before examining daily news reports of the proceedings and the opinion pieces they inspired.

The Defendants Call Americans Un-American

As the trial began, presiding Judge Julius Mayer warned the defendants that, although he would protect their rights, he would not allow any speeches in the courtroom. He would only entertain statements on the facts of the case.[17] Nonetheless, both Goldman and Berkman slipped their ideology into the court record whenever they could. Beginning with the jury selection, Goldman and Berkman infused references to their ideas about conscription—as well as such topics as birth control, women's emancipation, and religion—into the courtroom. Among the questions they asked the potential jurors was whether they believed in free speech and the right to criticize laws.[18] Certainly, within their lines of questioning, Goldman and Berkman sought to identify jurists who would be most sympathetic. At the same time, however, they were working toward Goldman's other goal—to use the court as a forum for anarchist beliefs.

Figure 4.1 Emma Goldman with her life-long comrade Alexander Berkman. Berkman injured his foot before the first No-Conscription League meeting and unsuccessfully attempted to have the federal court trial postponed because of it.

Source: National Archives.

Once the jury had been selected and sworn in, Berkman, who primarily spoke on the pair's behalf throughout the proceedings, addressed the court with arguments for dismissal of the case. He raised some legal arguments, stating, much like Weinberger did in his Supreme Court appeal, that he and Goldman did not commit a crime and the Selective Service Act was unconstitutional. However, most of his arguments dealt with the morality of conscription. Echoing No-Conscription League writings and speeches, he asserted that the people opposed war because human life is sacred. Thus, conscription forced people to act against their consciences. Furthermore, it forced American men to die on foreign soil against their wills, depriving them of the opportunity to die in their native land.[19] Berkman proclaimed, "we, defendants, take this opportunity to state clearly and frankly to you, gentlemen of the jury, that we are opposed to conscription." But he and Goldman denied that they had induced men not to register. The Selective Service Act excluded both defendants from registering; therefore, they did not feel they could advise anyone against it. Berkman and Goldman admitted, however, that they had been carrying on anti-militarist propaganda for more than twenty years, and they insisted that the speeches and writings for which they were being tried simply continued "the normal expression of opinions and activities" the defendants had conducted for decades without government interference.[20] The pair repeated their oft-told claims of war's capitalist purposes and oppression of the middle class, as well as their assertions that conscientious objectors were not slackers or cowards. Instead, Goldman proclaimed, they were brave souls willing to stand up against prevailing opinion "like a glittering lone star upon a dark horizon" and refuse to participate in murder.[21]

The duo also addressed the topic of anarchy. Because authorities could not demonstrate Berkman and Goldman had conspired to induce men not to register, the defendants surmised that anarchy really was what the government had put on trial. Both proudly admitted to being anarchists and aimed to explain what anarchy was about—and, more importantly, what it was not. They avowed that anarchy should not be equated with violence and denied that they encouraged violence. Berkman turned the allegation around on his accusers, averring that anyone who supported war favored wholesale violence. Anarchists did not believe in war; they believed in universal peace. Whereas belligerent nations murdering and slaughtering each other were destructive, anarchists were constructive because they believed in working together and helping each other. "Anarchism wants to change the false values of hatred, of strife, of brother murdering brother, the false values of exploitation and robbery, of tyranny, of oppression," Berkman explained. "We want to change these false values and give humanity new values." In fact, Berkman declared, he and Goldman were on trial for loving humanity. Their crime was standing up for the rights of exploited children, for equal rights of every women and every man, for the rights of the working class.[22]

Goldman averred that her rights and those of her comrade had been trampled throughout the legal process. She and Berkman had not wielded swords, guns, or bombs—only pens. Yet because they were anarchists, they were treated worse than felons. Authorities would provide most lawbreakers with warrants for search and seizure but did not provide them to Goldman and Berkman before turning their offices into a battlefield. Goldman compared the "good American patriots" who invaded and destroyed their private space to the Prussian barbarians who had done the same to Belgium. Furthermore, she asserted, authorities had demanded higher bail than was necessary for their alleged crime and refused to accept Berkman's property as bond, "thus breaking every right guaranteed even to the most heinous criminals." Finally, she contended that she and Berkman had not been given a fair trial. Instead, she insisted they had been tried on "a trumped-up charge" and defamed by "perjured testimony."[23] Though her ideas may be foreign, Goldman told the jury, she and Berkman were not the dangerous troublemakers the prosecutor and press made them out to be, any more than Jesus was a criminal for spreading His word or America's founding fathers were for framing the Declaration of Independence.[24]

Goldman denied that anarchy was un-American; she disputed that opposing war and conscription were disloyal to American principles. She proclaimed herself to be just as patriotic as the jurists hearing her arguments. She rejected the assumption that "the mere accident of birth in a certain country or the mere scrap of a citizen's paper constitutes the love of country." In fact, Goldman avowed that she and others who were not born in the United States "love America with deeper passion and greater intensity than many natives." While she loved the many beautiful things it had to offer, she hated its superficiality, corruption, and capitalism. By her words, she aimed to make America better. In particular, she hoped to open people's eyes to the hypocrisy of a government entering war to make the world safe for democracy when democracy was not safe in America. Goldman declared that "democracy at home is daily being outraged, free speech suppressed, peaceable assemblies broken up by overbearing and brutal gangsters in uniform" while "free press is curtailed and every independent opinion gagged."[25]

Goldman and Berkman believed free expression was a paramount necessity for liberty and democracy; thus, the defendants asserted their no-conscription activities should be protected. Those who indicted Berkman and Goldman for their speeches and what they published in *Mother Earth* and *The Blast* were the real criminals. In fact, Berkman implied that putting him and Goldman on trial for their expression was un-American. All other countries—even Russia—knew that free speech was sacred, Berkman contended. He decreed:

> I believe the moment you begin to limit free speech, the moment you begin to persecute those who believe in the use of free speech, that moment you are committing the worst crime against liberty, the worst crime against democracy, the worst crime against the traditions in which you believe, the worst crime against the best interests of the people.[26]

Berkman noted that he and Goldman had opened the platform at their meetings to anyone who wanted to speak and the pages of their publications to anyone who wanted to write, regardless of their opinions. Open discussion provided clarity, understanding, and sympathy, he avowed. Berkman believed the American people and government should do the same. Whether anarchy was correct or wrong, he and Goldman had a right to discuss their perspectives openly. If they were foolish, their ideas would be rejected and no harm would be done. If they were right, suppressing their ideas robbed the people of an opportunity to be enlightened.[27]

Berkman concluded that limiting free speech and discussion was more dangerous than the views he and Goldman espoused. Such suppression, he proclaimed, was "the assassination of liberty." The real question of the trial, then, was whether or not the people of America had free speech and liberty of expression. Berkman hoped the jury was "intelligent enough to know that this country was originally founded upon the liberty of conscience, upon free speech, upon the free expression and discussion of opinion."[28] Goldman and Berkman's orations totaled more than three hours, but only a small fraction of their words appeared in the mainstream press.[29] What appeared in the newspapers contrasted sharply with Goldman and Berkman's assertions that they were true Americans whereas their accusers were not.

Daily Trial Coverage

As the jury selection began, the reporters, with their waiting notebooks, carefully documented exchanges the defendants had with potential jury members, as well as the judge's reprimands when Goldman and Berkman strayed beyond what he believed were the reasonable limits of such questioning. A wire report that ran in at least a dozen newspapers after the second day of jury selection quoted Goldman as asking potential jurors, "Would you be prejudiced against the defendants to know that Emma Goldman had devoted a large part of her life to the emancipation of women?" and "Would you be prejudiced against Emma

ANARCHIST IS HIS OWN LAWYER

Emma Goldman Squelched by Judge When She Tries to "Butt In"

Figure 4.2 Much like other headlines on June 28 wire reports of the federal court trial, the *Reading* (PA) *Times* emphasized Judge Mayer putting Goldman in her place.

Goldman if it came out in the trial that she advocated birth control for the poor?"[30] Thus, these lines of questioning found their way into newspapers throughout the country. Such instances, however, were not as common as Goldman might have hoped or expected. While she was "determined to use [the trial] to best advantage" and to "wring from our enemies every chance to propagate our ideas," reporters and editors did not always cooperate.[31] Reporters' decisions regarding what to focus on from each day of the trial and editors' choices regarding headlines to pair with those stories often worked against Goldman's efforts.

The Associated Press report on the trial's opening day, which was published in newspapers throughout the nation on June 28, led with the charges that Goldman faced but emphasized a single moment from the day's proceedings. Berkman asked potential jurors if they were Christians, what they thought about patriotism, and what their social involvements were. The prosecutor objected to these lines of questioning for each potential juror, and Judge Mayer, growing tired of the pair's seemingly off-topic questioning, rebuked Berkman. Goldman stood, according to the story's description, and stated, "Your honor, may I say something?" Judge Mayer curtly responded, "No, sit down." The next paragraph simply reads, "She obeyed."[32] This exchange, selected from the full day's events in the courtroom, was the highlight in the AP report. Newspaper editors played on the exchange in their headlines. The Portland *Oregonian's* headline over the story simply read, "Emma Goldman Obeys"; the *Boston Herald*'s stated, "Tells Emma Goldman to Sit Down, and She Does."[33] Thus, as Goldman succeeded in some instances to be quoted as she spoke about her ideas, even in the form of questions to potential jurors, newspapers also framed the trial's coverage in ways that were dismissive of her ideas, generally presenting them as if they were unworthy of serious consideration. Furthermore, some coverage framed the government, via the judge, as finally putting Goldman in her place.

Despite these narratives, Goldman was most successful in converting the courtroom into a forum when reporters stuck to traditional journalistic conventions in writing fact-based leads and focusing on the events that transpired, which they often did. Woven into even the most even-handed reports, however, were nationalistic undercurrents and emphases on Goldman's otherness as a foreign-born visitor. As the AP did when relaying the jury-selection exchange, editors at times appeared to play to the crowd in the sense that they knew Goldman was massively unpopular within their readership; thus, they represented her in a way that would be well received. While these efforts to provide news the audience might want to hear were generally implicit and intermixed with more step-by-step trial coverage within the day-to-day trial reports, they were more explicitly emphasized in letters to the editor and editorial items, which are discussed later in this chapter.

Newspapers did not publish the defendants' most complete statements about freedom of expression and human rights. While their ideas about liberty and democracy were explored in *Mother Earth*, no mention of them was made in the wire reports that newspapers throughout the country relied upon as they brought their readers information from the trial.[34] Some of these types of omissions could be related to the amount of space the newspapers set aside for trial coverage. Reports from each day of the trial, which lasted from June 27 until July 9, were competing for space alongside often extensive coverage of the war and the war effort. Stories about wins and losses along the front, supply routes, government bonds, rationing, and the intake of draftees and their training and deployment dominated front pages and the overall column-inches available in newspapers across the country. Coverage of the first day of jury selection in the *New York Times*, for example, was slotted into page 5. To get to that story, readers would have encountered news that almost entirely pertained to the war. Furthermore, the headlines were universally supportive of the war. Some of the front-page headlines read "American Troops Reach France, Setting Record for Quick Movement," "1,400 More Enlist; Still Need 50,000," and "U-Boat Sinkings Show Falling Off from Last Week."[35] On page 4, opposite the *Times*'s coverage of Goldman's trial, headlines read, "Japan Hails America as Ally in the War," "Germans' Fat Rations for Next Winter Cut," and "Sees Eagle Strike German from Sky."[36] Similarly, on the second day of jury selection, the *Albuquerque Journal* placed Goldman's trial on its front page. Editors placed a picture of the secretary of the Navy and his son alongside the story, and the rest of the page was dominated by the headlines "Led in Rush on Germans; Gets a Commission" and "Washington is Waiting Report from Pershing."[37] Amidst the war news, newspapers devoted varying amounts of space to the trial reports. The wire services generally led with a boilerplate-style recitation of the defendant's names, the fact that they were anarchists, and their charges. This information often accounted for half or one-third of the overall space the story was given each day.[38] As a result, the first and final days of the trial yielded the best opportunity for Goldman to convey her ideas. These were the days in which the trial received the most attention.

While none of Goldman's impassioned speech about human liberty during her closing arguments found its way into the wire or New York newspapers' coverage, reports from the final day of the trial on July 10 included several extended quotes. Goldman, according to the reports, argued that she and Berkman were convicted "because we were anarchists. We were convicted with prejudice."[39] Although the newspapers did not discuss the defendants' views on free speech, they did include the judge's. Judge Mayer was quoted instructing the jury that the trial was not "a question of free speech for free speech is guaranteed to us under the constitution." He asserted, "No American worthy of the name believes in anything else than free speech, but free speech means not license, not counseling disobedience of the law." He continued by indicating that free speech must be lawful and orderly.[40] The *New York Times*'s coverage of the trial's final day included the documentation of a similar speech by Judge Mayer, though it was framed as part of the sentencing. The story reports that Judge Mayer indicated the government and its laws were created by the people and protected through the Civil War. He is quoted as stating, in terms that emphasized Goldman and Berkman's foreignness, "For such people as these, who would destroy our Government and nullify its laws, we have no place in this country."[41]

However, the *New York Times* story exposed readers to some of Goldman's views. It quoted her contending, "No matter what your verdict is it cannot have the least effect on the tremendous storm now brewing in the United States of America. Our verdict cannot affect the growing discontent in America."[42] Such a statement would appear to be an ideal representation of Goldman's efforts to spread her ideas via the courtroom forum. Another wire story, which ran in the *Trenton Evening News*, characterized Goldman as a "determined fighter." The story documented her request for a deferred sentence, which was denied, and the judge's lament, as the trial ended, that "the extraordinary ability of the two defendants," if used properly, could have helped to benefit the nation.[43] While the final day of the trial appears to have provided Goldman the greatest success in relaying her ideas, newspapers also covered Goldman and Berkman's efforts to communicate their beliefs early in the trial. The first paragraph of *New York Times* coverage at the trial's start outlined Goldman's efforts to "prove that anarchy is a beneficent 'social philosophy,'" and that she and Berkman had been "laboring to better the condition of the working class."[44]

These types of reports, however, were generally overshadowed by stories that focused on the spectacle of the trial or trivialized Goldman's efforts. Two stories focused on Goldman's refusal to stand for the National Anthem when it could be heard in the court room from a nearby park. In addition, three of Goldman's supporters were removed from the courtroom for refusing to stand. One story led with,

> For the second time since Emma Goldman and Alexander Berkman, anarchists, have been on trial in the federal court at New York for conspiracy to obstruct operation of the selective draft law, several of their radical sympathizers were ejected from the courtroom.[45]

Thus, in the passage, the report was fact-based, but it also betrayed skepticism toward Goldman's ideas. Furthermore, it emphasized Goldman's foreignness, identifying her as an immigrant who had failed to accept patriotic practices—the type of immigrant Roosevelt and others asserted should be barred from the country. As if to further isolate Goldman from American readers, newspapers associated her with the hated Germans. Wire stories about the third day of the trial, June 30, raised questions about whether German spies funded Goldman's activities.[46] However, the newspapers did not follow up on these reports with more information about how these questions were answered in the courtroom, where the rumors of authorities finding receipts for German money in the *Mother Earth* office were dispelled as fake news.[47]

In stark contrast to portrayals of Goldman as un-American, the *Charlotte Observer* ran a lengthy story about a Kentucky man who interrupted one of the final days of the trial to secure custody of his son, who had been arrested for refusing to register for the draft. The story extensively quoted the father about his love for the United States and his promise that his son would register for the draft, assuring that "if he don't [*sic*], something will happen in the public square back home." The story ends with the father referring to Goldman and Berkman, explaining, "we don't have folks like that out our way." In this way, the report juxtaposed the father—a humble, hard-working American who was willing to offer his son to the war effort without any reservation—with Goldman and Berkman, radical foreigners accused of impeding the draft process. Unlike portrayals of Goldman in nearly every report during the trial, the newspaper quoted the father in long blocks and framed him as a patriot.[48]

Other stories focused on the death threats the judge and district attorney faced, how many guards were assigned to secure the courtroom, and how Goldman's supporters dressed and behaved.[49] The New York *Sun's* coverage of the trial was particularly dismissive of Goldman's ideas, retelling developments in the courtroom as if they were turning points in a sporting event. The lead in the July 3 report indicated, "The stalwart men of the law had on the preceding days marked up several points against some of the low belted, smock enclosed, sandaled young friends of Emma."[50] Despite this tone, the report later conveyed Berkman's argument against the Selective Service Act, quoting his argument, "The conscription law is unconstitutional. It is a violation of the moral, ethical and religious views of the people of the United States. The conscription law is highly immoral and prejudicial to the best interest of the country."[51]

Finally, the trial coverage identified journalists Lincoln Steffens and John Reed, as well as Free Speech League President Leonard Abbott and member Bolton Hall, an activist and lawyer, as witnesses who testified on Goldman's behalf. The stories, however, included little that pertained to Goldman and what was said about her or her ideas. Judge Mayer engaged Hall in an extended discussion about freedom of expression. After Hall testified that he was a member of the Free Speech League, Judge Mayer asked him what he meant. Hall explained, "It believes in activities tending to promote liberty, and particularly free speech. We have long fought for free speech."[52] Judge Mayer asked if free speech meant violating existing statutes. Hall responded, "I think that is free speech." As for Goldman, Hall testified that he had never known her to be violent or to advocate violence. Berkman argued before the court that witnesses such as Hall, Steffens, Reed, and Abbott were of the "best caliber." In questioning Steffens, Goldman established how long they had known each other, which she recalled was more than twenty years. She then asked him whether he had ever heard her, in public or private, advocate for violence. He answered "no."[53]

Very little regarding these witnesses' testimonies was reported. The *New York Tribune* report, reprinted in the *Kansas City Star* under the

Figure 4.3 This 1914 news service photograph depicts American journalist Lincoln Steffens, one of the witnesses who testified on Goldman's behalf, sitting at Union Square—the site of the 1893 and 1916 speeches for which Goldman was prosecuted.

Source: Library of Congress.

headline "Fun at the Trial of Anarchists," focused on a long joke that Reed told about his own arrest and Steffens jostling about the types of questions Berkman asked him.[54] A report about Abbott's time at the trial focused on his conclusion that he was disappointed the first time he heard Goldman speak. The story quoted Abbott as stating he expected a "stronger and more definite" speech.[55] The final portion of the same story depicted Berkman and Goldman as violent radicals, conveying that the prosecution provided the jury with several speeches in which Berkman and Goldman spoke of "dynamite and bombs."[56] This report was contrary to the defendants' assertions and the statements of their witnesses that anarchists were not violent. The newspapers did not include Berkman's speech regarding anarchists as pacifists or the defendants' denial that they ever encouraged violence in their speeches or writings.[57]

Thus, newspaper readers generally encountered reports framed to support the government's case against Goldman and Berkman and reinforce their otherness as immigrants who communicated unpopular ideas. Reporters, in some instances, conveyed Goldman's perspective. In many others, however, they focused more on the trial as a form of spectacle or on the fact that the two defendants were anarchists. Their arguments regarding freedom of expression received little attention in the newspapers. The wire services and major New York newspapers did not report her impassioned final arguments, and the lone focus on free speech during the trial came from Judge Mayer, who defined the right in a way that excluded Goldman's speech from protection. Judge Mayer's definition of free expression was not an aberration, however. While the Supreme Court's first major free expression cases were right around the corner in 1919, Judge Mayer's limited views were strongly shared by readers and editors in the opinion sections of newspapers throughout the trial. Importantly, considering these daily trial stories without examining the opinion pieces that were published in papers at the time paints a limited picture of the discourse that surrounded the proceedings.

Cutting Quips and Thoughtful Reflections

Goldman's trial took place as the first American troops were arriving in France and thousands of draftees were leaving their families to enter boot camps for short, intensive training before shipping off to Europe. Often on the same days that newspapers included news about Goldman's trial, much of the front page was devoted to the war. On the day that Goldman was convicted, for example, her trial's news ran on the top left of the *New York Times*'s front page. Much of the top right of the page was devoted to war news such as "Russians Take 7,131 Men, 48 Guns," and "Kaiser Is Now Arranging to Hold a Crown Council."[58] This dichotomy between Goldman—who fought against government and believed that forced conscription was antithetical to human liberty—and the nation's ramping up for the "war to end all wars" was not lost on newspaper readers, columnists, and editorial-page editors around the country. Newspapers often included stark, mean-spirited, and, at times, relatively constructive discussions of Goldman and her beliefs. These ideas commonly connected Goldman's trial with other events happening in the world. They also emphasized, in a far more explicit way than was evidenced in the day-to-day trial coverage, that Goldman was generally understood as an "other"—someone who was foreign-born, whom Americans once had accepted but now rejected. These opinion pieces showed strong civic nationalism, focusing on Goldman's failure to support American values. In many instances, more so than in the daily trial coverage, publishers interwove free speech concerns into their arguments, particularly as they related to a time of war.

A Worn-Out Welcome

Pieces that appeared in newspaper opinion pages consistently positioned Goldman as a visitor who had benefited from Americans' graciousness and decency only to abuse the kindness offered to her. She was, to these letter-writers, columnists, and editorial boards, the guest that misused the nation's hospitality. Many of the pieces went a step further, arguing that Goldman should be deported because she had worn out her warm welcome. In an editorial headlined "Jailed 'Philosophers,'" *The San Diego Evening News* reasoned that Goldman sought and found a warm reception to the United States because "our gates are ever wide to the reception of outcasts of all lands." Of course, the author continued by indicating that Goldman was among many outcasts who had come to this nation and therefore had made the United States "largely populated by ignorant and illiterate immigrants who never knew the meaning of the word 'liberty.'" The editorial highlighted that Goldman and Berkman were not American citizens, concluding that they acted as "snakes that have squirmed in the grass of our political preserve, despised, perhaps, but hitherto unhindered save as they were driven from place to place by righteously indignant communities." The author's solution, as was the case with most, was to call for Goldman to be deported.[59] San Diego in general, and the *Evening News* in particular, never had tolerated Goldman's ideas. She and her companion Ben Reitman were barred from speaking at a San Diego event in 1912, a move that the *Evening News* encouraged and justified as an acceptable limitation on expression.[60] With the consent of San Diego authorities, anti-IWW vigilantes kidnapped and tortured Reitman; he was beaten, tarred, and burned.[61]

North of San Diego, the *San Jose Mercury News*'s opinion page carried a similarly themed editorial on the same day as the *Evening News*'s. The piece also focused on what the United States had given Goldman, and how she had abused it. The author wrote, "One would suppose that the very freedom the woman has enjoyed in America … might soften her attitude toward society, but she sought not partial but complete realization of her dreams."[62] The author continued, later in the piece, by highlighting that, while the United States never had been perfect, it had "done so much for its masses. Here the plainest man may live in peace and plenty; his children enjoy the training which the country affords without money and without price." The final paragraph contended that the country offered all of these benefits to Goldman, but she *chose* to reject them.[63]

Other newspapers were less nuanced. A column in Michigan's *Bay City Times* emphasized that Goldman and Berkman had "abused the privileges of this country" and "made themselves obnoxious," citing as

Figure 4.4 A special San Diego issue of *Mother Earth*, published after Ben Reitman's ordeal, depicts "patriotic" vigilantes crushing free speech.

Source: HathiTrust Digital Library.

evidence a list of Goldman's arrests and convictions.[64] A lengthy editorial in Illinois's *Belleville Democrat* on July 10 similarly emphasized that Goldman was not an American and that she, Berkman, and Reitman had attacked "the State and the Church and established society and the general discussion of public questions and public men from the socialistic and anarchistic point of view." The piece ended by applauding Goldman's prison sentence and advocating that she be deported when her time had been served.[65] Similarly, a letter to the editor in the *Salt Lake Telegram* emphasized America's "good natured public" had to draw the line somewhere with Goldman, and once the war started, she had to be locked up.[66] Finally, after Goldman's sentencing, the *Oregonian* concluded, "She finds that the nation which has protected her proposes, first of all, to protect itself."[67] The conclusion was far more eloquent than the *Lexington Herald's* twenty-two-word quip, which read, "Emma Goldman says, 'I would rather be shot than shoot,' which makes it unanimous with all those who know that little devil."[68] In each of these instances, newspaper opinion pages conveyed the idea that Goldman, despite being warmly received and gifted with the freedoms that the United States offered her, had rejected them and thus should be punished.

Not One of Us

The narrative conveyed within opinion pieces that were published during and immediately after Goldman's trial commonly depicted her as an other, someone who did not share the beliefs, goals, and values that defined Americans. Furthermore, the items often raised concerns that Goldman's rhetoric could induce others to turn away from these same cherished values. Thus, the pieces often created an *us-versus-her* dichotomy. This theme is not significantly different from the idea in the preceding section that she was a visitor who had worn out her welcome. In both instances, the opinion pieces implicitly or explicitly identified certain American values and found Goldman to be lacking in them. The authors then used their findings to justify why Goldman's expression should be halted, her prison sentence supported, and her deportation planned. A short opinion item in the *Philadelphia Inquirer* emphasized that a government is "founded on law and order" and that citizens should not "obstruct the formation of armies to fight the common enemy of humanity." The author asserted that "there is no room in a free country for such miserable creatures as Alexander Berkman and Emma Goldman and their murderous tribe." Thus, the essay conveyed, rather explicitly, that Goldman was part of a different tribe, and that tribe did not share the nation's values. The author specifically celebrated law and order, freedom, and humanity—all values that Americans possessed and Goldman did not.[69]

Similarly, an editorial in the *Belleville Democrat* explained that Goldman and Berkman threatened "everything which good men and the great masses of the people deem necessary for the preservation of social order." The item proclaimed that Goldman used her speeches, pamphlets, and "a red-flag periodical" to "keep up agitation against the government and the existing order." Ultimately, the editorial concluded that "America only fights in righteous causes, for justice, for liberty and for the eternal rights of man. With America right is might." Goldman, in the argument that is constructed, opposed these crucial, society-supporting ideals, and thus should be silenced.[70] A column in the *Bay City Times* drew upon similar reasoning. The author asserted that Goldman and Berkman had set an "incorrect example to others of their nationality who were easily influenced by their words" and "trodden on statutes which have been designed to protect the people of this country."[71] An item in the *Oregonian*, which was headlined "Fair Warning," emphasized that Goldman's conviction should send a message to others like her. The piece outlined Goldman's history of defying the law, acting in contempt, undermining social order, and encouraging men not to enlist. The item, in its conclusion, noted that "there are other public nuisances who ought to find in the Goldman–Berkman convictions full and fair warning. The temper of the United States – which means the Government, which also means the people – is quite sensitive."[72] Thus, in these instances, limiting Goldman and Berkman's expression was rationalized because the ideas they communicated did not align with the dominant socially accepted norms at the time.

These justifications regarding protecting social order and national security are particularly interesting when placed within the historical development of freedom of expression in the United States, which is examined in greater detail in Chapter 2. Up to this point, the Supreme Court had never squarely addressed freedom of expression. While the Supreme Court declined to draw upon First Amendment arguments in rejecting Goldman's appeal in 1918, several similar cases that dealt with expression against the United States's efforts in the war followed her appeal. By the end of 1919, the Supreme Court, much as these opinion pieces were doing in 1917, was constructing rationales and limits for freedom of expression. In *Schenck v. United States*, for example, the Court concluded that freedom of expression could be halted if it represented a clear and present danger. Such an approach bears similarities to the authors' arguments that Goldman's ideas were a danger to social institutions and norms.

No Free Speech in War Time

The opinion pieces not only concluded that Goldman's actions and beliefs separated her from the American values and institutions that were crucial to society, thus making her expression something that could be limited; the columns, letters to the editor, and editorials also rationalized limiting her expression by reasoning that her messages might pose a danger to the nation during wartime. Interestingly, this theme was also a significant part of Justice Oliver Wendell Holmes's opinion for the Court in *Schenck*, where he reasoned that,

> When a nation is at war many things that might be said in times of peace are such a hindrance to its effort that their utterance will not be endured so long as men fight and that no Court could regard them as protected by any constitutional right.[73]

In opinion pieces throughout the nation during Goldman's trial, writers called upon similar justifications in their arguments against her rights. An editorial in the *Dallas Morning News*, published at the start of the proceedings, questioned the sincerity of her and Berkman's beliefs and advocated for the pair to be locked up during the duration of the war, whether they were guilty of the crimes they were accused of or not. The editorial explained that Goldman and Berkman "have long been more of a nuisance to the country. Their anarchy has been more profitable to themselves than dangers to society." The editorial continued, however, by explaining that in peacetime, the country could possibly tolerate them, but "just now the country can not well afford to be distracted and annoyed by them."[74] Quite similarly, a letter to the editor that ran in the *Salt Lake Telegram* celebrated the importance of free speech and free press as rights that Americans guard carefully. However, the letter explained that "now we are at war. The government represents the people and the citizenships of this democratic republic." The author, who signed the letter "subscriber," asserted "the time has come for treasonable editors and orators to shut up or be locked up."[75]

The authors of these opinion pieces consistently equated Goldman's speech with treason or sedition rather than protected expression. An editorial in the *Belleville Democrat* reasoned, "People like Goldman and Berkman claim the right of free speech," but avowed there was no such thing. "To oppose the government in wartime is treason," the author proclaimed, "and treason is a crime." The same item indicated that the time to discuss the war ended when the war started, which aligned with sentiments in other publications.[76] For instance, an editorial that ran the following day in the *Oregonian* emphasized that "it is no time now to deal leniently with the Goldmans and the Berkmans, or with any of the voices of treason and lawlessness."[77] Similarly, on the same day, the *San Jose Mercury News* published an editorial that separated Goldman's ideas from free speech. The piece contended that she is "not going to prison for speaking freely, but because her words were seditiously calculated to impair confidence in the government."[78] Essentially, these authors avowed that the ideas Goldman expressed were not a form of free expression because they represented a danger to the nation. They communicated that the peril was particularly great during a time of war. Finally, in the most explicit version of this theme, the author of a letter to the editor in the *Boston Journal* on July 5 concluded that he "would suspend free speech in war times." He reasoned that

> Berkman and Goldman are a distinct menace in times of peace; in war they are dangerous to the welfare of our armies in the field. They should be locked up until our soldiers have returned – all of them – from the firing line.[79]

Together these opinion pieces constructed a narrative that was substantially similar to the reasoning put forth by the Supreme Court two years later, in its earliest efforts to interpret the First Amendment's promises of freedom of expression. As the Court would reason in *Schenck* and reinforce in *Abrams v. United States* later in 1919, freedom of expression can receive different protections during a time of war or uncertainty than it does in times of peace.[80] Justice Holmes explained,

> The question in every case is whether the words used are used in such circumstances and are of such a nature as to create a clear and present danger that they will bring about the substantive evils that Congress has a right to prevent.[81]

Interestingly, despite the lack of attention that freedom of speech received from the Court in Goldman's appeal before the Supreme Court in December 1917, Justice Holmes cited the justices' opinion in that case within this passage in *Schenck*, providing some limited evidence that perhaps the most esteemed jurist in the nation's history ultimately did correlate Goldman's case as a freedom-of-expression concern.

Ultimately, Goldman's efforts to use media coverage of her trial as an avenue through which to disseminate her ideas throughout the nation had the unintended consequence of creating a conversation about freedom of expression within newspaper opinion pages. Mixed within this conversation, however, were nationalism-related themes, which focused on Goldman's otherness as an immigrant who had taken advantage of Americans' kindness. In the opinion pages, however, Goldman's ideas were discussed and tested, despite the skepticism they faced. The opinion pieces questioned the amount of tolerance a nation should have for unpopular ideas and the potential boundaries of free speech. The daily coverage of Goldman's trial proved to be less fruitful as few of her ideas reached readers. Goldman's calculated decision to represent herself, however, likely yielded more discussion of her ideas within daily papers' pages than if she had not.

Notes

1 "Emma Goldman Locked Up," *Boston Herald*, June 16, 1917; "Noted 'Reds' Under Arrest in New York," *Idaho Statesman* (Boise), June 16, 1917; "Nab Anarchists as Draft Foes Emma Goldman and Alexander Berkman Seized in Raid by Federal Agents," *Kalamazoo* (MI) *Gazette*, June 16, 1917.
2 "Emma Goldman and A. Berkman Behind the Bars," *New York Times*, June 16, 1917.
3 *United States v. Goldman & Berkman*: Indictment, District Court of the United States, for the Southern District of New York, June 1917, in Candace Falk, with Ronald J. Zboray, et al., eds., *The Emma Goldman Papers: A Microfilm Edition* (Alexandria, VA: Chadwyck-Healey, Inc., 1990; hereafter referred to as Goldman Papers), reel 57.
4 Emma Goldman, *Living My Life* (Garden City, NY: Garden City Publishing, 1934), 611.
5 Ibid.; "Trial and Speeches of Alexander Berkman and Emma Goldman in the United States in District Court, in the City of New York, July 1917" (New York: Mother Earth Publishing Association, 1917), 11, Goldman Papers, reel 57.
6 Goldman, *Living My Life*, 612–613; "Bond for Two Anarchists is Made $25,000," *Fort Worth* (TX) *Star-Telegram*, June 17, 1917; "Goldman and Berkman are Held to Federal Jury," *Grand Forks* (ND) *Daily Herald,* June 17, 1917.
7 Goldman, *Living My Life*, 612–613. Goldman wrote friends asking them to wire as much money as they could. See Emma Goldman to Agnes Inglis (telegram), June 21, 1917, and Emma Goldman to Ellen Kennan (telegram), June 22, 1917, Goldman Papers, reel 10.
8 Emma Goldman to Agnes Inglis, June 29, 1917, Goldman Papers, reel 10.
9 Goldman, *Living My Life*, 613–614.
10 Ibid., 603.
11 Ibid.
12 See, for example, "Emma Goldman and Alex Berkman Arrested," *Dallas Morning News*, June 16, 1917; "Noted 'Reds' Under Arrest in New York"; "Emma Goldman is Locked Up," *Miami Herald*, June 16, 1917.
13 "Emma Goldman and A. Berkman Behind the Bars"; "Berkman and Emma Goldman Held for Plot," *Sun* (New York), June 16, 1917; "Emma Goldman and Berkman Arrested," *New York Tribune*, June 16, 1917.
14 "Emma Goldman and A. Berkman Behind the Bars."
15 "Berkman and Emma Goldman Held for Plot."
16 *Tulsa Daily World*, July 2, 1917.

17 *United States v. Goldman & Berkman*: Stenographer's Notes, District Court of the United States, for the Southern District of New York, June 1917, 9, Goldman Papers, reel 58.
18 "Trial and Speeches of Alexander Berkman and Emma Goldman," 12–13.
19 *United States v. Goldman & Berkman*: Stenographer's Notes, 14.
20 "Trial and Speeches of Alexander Berkman and Emma Goldman," 31.
21 Ibid., 59.
22 Ibid., 32–36.
23 Ibid., 56–57.
24 Ibid., 62.
25 Ibid., 63–64.
26 Ibid., 49–50.
27 Ibid., 50.
28 Ibid.
29 Goldman, *Living My Life*, 621.
30 "Berkman Again Annoys Judge by Questions Asked," *Albuquerque Morning Journal*, June 29, 1917.
31 Goldman, *Living My Life*, 615.
32 "Berkman Tries to Argue with Court," *Rockford* (IL) *Morning Star*, June 28, 1917.
33 "Emma Goldman Obeys," *Oregonian* (Portland, OR), June 28, 1917; "Tells Emma Goldman to Sit Down and She Does," *Boston Herald*, June 28, 1917.
34 For example, the August 1917 issue of *Mother Earth*, published a month after the trial ended, contained multiple articles on these themes. See "Observations and Comments," 194; Abbott, "The War Hysteria and Our Protest," 202–206; Martha Gruening, "Speaking of Democracy," 213–218.
35 *New York Times*, June 28, 1917.
36 Ibid.
37 *Albuquerque Journal*, June 29, 1917.
38 See, for example, "Government Closes Case Against Emma Goldman and Alexander Berkman," *Augusta Chronicle*, July 4, 1917; "Berkman Speaks Roughly," *News and Courier* (Charleston, SC), July 6, 1917; "Driven from Courtroom," *Richmond Times Dispatch*, July 7, 1917.
39 "Emma Goldman Sentenced to 2 Years in Prison," *Albuquerque Morning Journal*, July 10, 1917. The same report ran in several other newspapers: "Emma Goldman Going to Penitentiary," *Riverside* (CA) *Independent*, July 10, 1917; "Emma Goldman and Berkman Each Get Two-Year Sentence," *San Diego Union*, July 10, 1917; "Two Years in the Pen and $10,000 for Emma Goldman," *Columbus* (GA) *Daily Enquirer*, July 10, 1917; "Emma Goldman to Prison," *Kansas City Star*, July 10, 1917.
40 "Emma Goldman Sentenced to 2 Years in Prison."
41 "Convict Berkman and Goldman; Both off to Prison," *New York Times*, July 10, 1917.
42 Ibid. Goldman was speaking about discontent against war and opposition to conscription; see "Trial and Speeches of Alexander Berkman and Emma Goldman," 64.
43 "Goldman-Berkman Sentence, 2 Years," *Trenton Evening News*, July 10, 1917.
44 "Reds are Defiant, Can Get No Delay," *New York Times*, June 28, 1917.

45 "Eject Radicals," *Springfield Republican*, July 7, 1917. See also, "Driven from Courtroom," *Richmond Times*, July 7, 1917.
46 "Complete a Jury," *Tampa Tribune*, June 30, 1917; "Emma Goldman to be Asked Source of Money, " *Fort Worth Star-Telegram*, June 29, 1917.
47 During the trial, an eighty-year-old Swedish man testified that he had given Emma Goldman the mysterious check that authorities hinted was from German sources. Goldman assumed someone in the Marshal's office "told newspapers the fake story of German money." See "Trial and Speeches of Alexander Berkman and Emma Goldman," 15, 61.
48 "Raised His Boys to be Soldiers," *Charlotte Observer*, July 8, 1917.
49 See, for example, "Judge, Lawyer Get Death Threat if Reds are Tried," *Salt Lake City Telegram*, July 8, 1917.
50 " 'Reds' vs. U.S. Game Stands at a Draw," *Sun* (New York), July 3, 1917.
51 Ibid.
52 "Trial and Speeches of Alexander Berkman and Emma Goldman," 15.
53 *United States v. Goldman & Berkman*: Stenographer's Notes, 376–380.
54 "Fun at Trial of Anarchists," *Kansas City Star*, July 11, 1917.
55 "Emma Goldman was Too Mild for Abbot," *The Evening Times* (Pawtucket, RI), July 6, 1917.
56 Ibid.
57 See "Trial and Speeches of Alexander Berkman and Emma Goldman," 48, 58–59.
58 *New York Times*, July 10, 1917.
59 "Jailed 'Philosophers'," *San Diego Evening News*, July 11, 1917.
60 David M. Rabban, *Free Speech in the Forgotten Years* (Cambridge: Cambridge University Press, 1997), 118–119.
61 Goldman, *Living My Life,* 494–503.
62 "Fate of Emma Goldman," *San Jose Mercury News*, July 11, 1917.
63 Ibid.
64 "Justice Wakes Up," *Bay City* (MI) *Times*, July 11, 1917.
65 "Pathological Troublemakers and Copperheads Must Go to Prison," *Belleville* (IL) *Democrat*, July 10, 1917.
66 "Shut Up or be Locked Up," *Salt Lake Telegram*, July 2, 1917.
67 "Fair Warning," *Oregonian*, July 11, 1917.
68 Editorial, *Lexington Herald*, July 6.
69 "To Jail with the Anarchists," *Philadelphia Inquirer*, July 11, 1917.
70 "Pathological Troublemakers and Copperheads Must Go to Prison."
71 "Justice Wakes Up."
72 "Fair Warning."
73 *Schenck v. United States*, 249 U.S. 47, 52 (1919).
74 *Dallas Morning News*, June 28, 1917.
75 "Shut Up or Be Locked Up."
76 "Pathological Troublemakers and Copperheads Must Go to Prison."
77 "Fair Warning."
78 "The Fate of Emma Goldman."
79 "Would Suspend Free Speech in War Times," *Boston Journal*, July 5, 1917.
80 *Schenck v. United States*, 249 U.S. 47, 52 (1919).
81 Ibid.

5 Epilogue: The Spark

Judge Julius Mayer, presiding over Goldman and Berkman's federal court trial, asserted that people had the right to debate the Selective Service Act as vehemently as they desired before it was passed, but once it became law, they were duty-bound to obey it. He instructed the jury not to deliberate on the defendants' philosophies but only consider the evidence of the case, deciding whether the duo had, beyond a reasonable doubt, committed the crime for which they were accused. After forty minutes of deliberation, the jury returned with a guilty verdict.[1] Goldman and Berkman were each sentenced to two years in federal prison and fined $10,000; Goldman began serving her time at the Missouri State Penitentiary after the Supreme Court upheld her conviction.[2]

Mother Earth responded to the federal court ruling in its August 1917 issue with two essays. In one, Free Speech League Chairman Leonard Abbott insisted that the government had violated the inalienable rights of free speech, assemblage, and press because of the war hysteria; in the other, Goldman averred that *Mother Earth* quickly would recover from the plunder of its office. To Goldman, the magazine was a voice "imbued with high purpose and noble aim" that "no government can silence."[3] But the government did silence it; postal officials ruled the publication unmailable under the Espionage Act, and the August issue was its last.[4] Goldman lamented that the death of *Mother Earth* hurt her more than any prison sentence could. "No offspring of flesh and blood could absorb its mother as this child had drained me," she later wrote. "A struggle of over a decade, exhausting tours for its support, much worry and grief, had gone into the maintenance of *Mother Earth*, and now with one blow, its life had been snuffed out!"[5] In a September letter to subscribers announcing the magazine's demise, Goldman also expressed "indignation toward the war hysteria which has destroyed Free Press and Speech in America."[6]

Goldman's niece Stella Comyn and Berkman's lover Eleanor Fitzgerald operated an anemic newsletter version entitled *Mother Earth*

Bulletin in the magazine's place for six months. Goldman penned an introduction for the October 1917 issue lambasting the Postmaster General—"the absolute dictator over the press"—and indicating that the climate had made it impossible for "any publication with character" to be circulated. "As *Mother Earth* will not comply with these regulations and will not appear in an emasculated form," she explained, "it prefers to take a long needed rest until the world has regained its sanity." The *Bulletin* would, in the meantime, keep friends and subscribers posted about "our movements and activities."[7] The October issue also copied a letter Reitman wrote to the Postmaster General, asserting that the government denied *Mother Earth* mailing privileges simply because of its anarchist tenor and association with Goldman. But, Reitman argued, a free press was crucial to democracy, and according to the Constitution, no judge or postal official could decide what press was free. "We ask for our constitutionally guaranteed right to voice our grievances and to help build a world without tyranny, injustice and exploitation," Reitman declared.[8] The letter had no effect. Eventually, postal officials denied *Mother Earth Bulletin* the ability to circulate by mail, too. They also quickly shut down the *Bulletin*'s successor, a mimeographed circular entitled "Instead of a Magazine."[9] New York Postmaster Robert Bowen wrote to a superior that the "circular letter of the ill-smelling Mother Earth people should not be given the freedom of the mail." Bowen noted that the letter expressed "fulsome praise of 'Our Emma' Goldman and Alexander Berkman, and sympathy with them in their most deserved imprisonment." He reasoned that by publishing the circular in place of the forbidden *Bulletin*, *Mother Earth*'s publishers were dodging the ruling of the law, "and I cannot see why we should submit to it."[10]

In addition to updates on prison life, Goldman contributed essays on the Russian Revolution to the *Mother Earth Bulletin* during its short life.[11] Its demise robbed Goldman of her preferred forum, but she found other ways to express herself, particularly letters to her friends and fellow anarchists from prison. "Censorships had taught me to express proscribed ideas in guileless disguise," she later wrote, specifically noting discussions with IWW attorney Jacob Margolis about the pros and cons of Soviet Russia.[12] However, prison officials kept close tabs on her mail, too. Some letters—both incoming and outgoing—were turned over to immigration authorities as evidence of Goldman's anarchist beliefs.[13] In general, Goldman's prison experience was difficult. Before beginning her sentence, she expressed that she did not fear imprisonment because public life "under the present war hysteria" was just as bad, and she would prefer to be locked up than "MUZZLED in freedom."[14] However, Goldman was not able to keep her spirits as high in the penitentiary as she predicted. According to historian Bonnie Stepenoff, the prison system was not built for women because so few were incarcerated

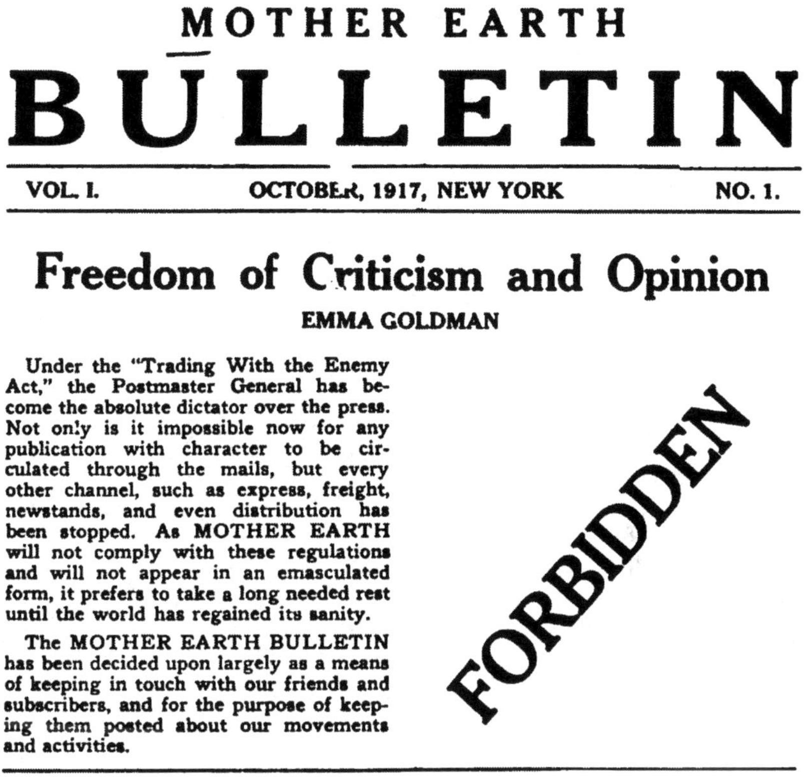

MOTHER EARTH

BULLETIN

VOL. I. OCTOBER, 1917, NEW YORK NO. 1.

Freedom of Criticism and Opinion

EMMA GOLDMAN

Under the "Trading With the Enemy Act," the Postmaster General has become the absolute dictator over the press. Not only is it impossible now for any publication with character to be circulated through the mails, but every other channel, such as express, freight, newstands, and even distribution has been stopped. As MOTHER EARTH will not comply with these regulations and will not appear in an emasculated form, it prefers to take a long needed rest until the world has regained its sanity.

The MOTHER EARTH BULLETIN has been decided upon largely as a means of keeping in touch with our friends and subscribers, and for the purpose of keeping them posted about our movements and activities.

FORBIDDEN

Figure 5.1 The first issue of *Mother Earth Bulletin* featured harsh commentary on suppressive wartime laws.

Source: HathiTrust Digital Library.

at the time. Women in Missouri's state penitentiary endured "a malignant neglect that made their position even more wretched than that of their male counterparts."[15] Within a year, Goldman felt broken. As she celebrated her fiftieth birthday in a jail cell, she contemplated whether her decades "in the firing line" had made any difference. She noted how much prison had aged her, as had "the savage persecution of radicals in America."[16]

Though Goldman left the confines of the Missouri State Penitentiary in September 1919, she was not free. J. Edgar Hoover himself had called for her deportation in an August memo to John T. Creighton, special assistant to the attorney general. Hoover labeled Goldman and Berkman "two of the most dangerous anarchists in the country" and predicted that allowing them to return to American society after their imprisonment would "result in undue harm."[17] Secretary of Labor John Abercrombie issued a warrant for Goldman's arrest as an alien anarchist on September 5; Weinberger posted $15,000 bond on her behalf so she did not have to remain in custody until her deportation hearing. He also submitted evidence of her citizenship.[18] Goldman never went through naturalization proceedings herself; she staked her claim to U.S. citizenship on her marriage in 1887 to Jacob Kershner, a naturalized Russian immigrant she had met while working at a garment factory in Rochester. Though they had been estranged for years, Goldman argued their marriage still was legal. However, authorities had revoked Kershner's citizenship in 1909, claiming he had not lived in the country the required five years when he was naturalized. Thus, immigration officials concluded, Goldman's citizenship was nullified as well. They also denied that she could claim citizenship because her father had been naturalized, given that she was not a minor when his naturalization occurred.[19]

On October 27, 1919, Goldman stood before immigration officials. Newspaper articles published before and during her trial two years earlier indicated that Goldman's views were intolerable to many. Hostility toward Goldman did not wane during her imprisonment. The Red Scare followed on the heels of the "war hysteria," thus rendering the Russian-born Goldman's radical perspective even more dangerous. An editorial from the *Minneapolis Journal* echoed the language of opinion pieces published during her federal trial. After a discussion about the distribution of Bolshevik propaganda by another radical, the essay asserted that Goldman's deportation should have followed her release from prison immediately. The writer wondered, "is there any reason why she should not be sent back to her native Russia, since she is so dissatisfied with the country that has long given her shelter?"[20] The *Ohio State Journal* referenced Goldman's deportation case in a column that asserted, "Every loyal American will be expected to stand behind the government in its efforts to ship these trouble-making anarchists out of the country." The writer believed it was unwise to "permit their disloyal ranting" in the past, "but it would be indefensible, now that the war has been fought for free government, to permit these people to continue their tactics."[21]

Immigration officials concurred. Goldman's hearing included a parade of evidence that she was an anarchist whose beliefs posed a danger to America: back issues of *Mother Earth* and other anarchist publications for which she had written and transcripts of former speeches.[22] She knew what the hearing's outcome would be and thus refused to participate in the "farce" by answering officials' questions. Instead, she used the hearing—as she had previous trials—as a forum for her beliefs. In her statement, Goldman rebuked tyranny and defended the people's rights to true democracy and liberty, including free speech. "The free expression of the hopes and aspirations of a people is the greatest and only safety in a sane society," she declared. "In truth, it is such free expression and discussion alone that can point the most beneficial path for human progress and development." Deportations under restrictionist laws that discriminated against radicals stifled the voice of the people, she asserted.[23]

Against the advice of Weinberger and others, while Goldman awaited news on immigration officials' decision, she publicly protested the discriminatory arrest and deportation of Russians and radical sympathizers. Whereas the former belligerent nations in Europe had granted political amnesty to enemy aliens, "America alone failed to open her prison doors." After the Palmer raids, Goldman received numerous requests to lecture on the "Federal deportation mania" that was "terrorizing the foreign workers of the country."[24] Because of potent anti-radical fervor in New York, officials prevented Goldman from securing any meeting space there.[25] However, she—along with Berkman and Margolis—spoke to audiences of thousands in Detroit and Chicago, under the watchful eye of local authorities and Federal agents.[26] Speaking at the hall of an automobile and aircraft workers' union, Goldman pronounced herself "infinitely more American" than the so-called patriots of the American Legion and other organizations. Similar to her arguments during her federal trial in 1917, Goldman asserted that native-born Americans were American by compulsion, but she was American by choice, because "like many foolish and deluded foreigners I believed that America is the promised land." She declared the America that had accumulated "untold fortunes out of the sweat and blood of the millions of the people who came to their shores" was a different America than what the nation's forefathers conceived; the founders of the republic "would turn in their graves if they could see what their children and great-grandchildren have made of the wonderful gift which they have given the world."[27]

Goldman lamented that the Russian boys whom federal agents attacked in the November 7 Palmer raids had done nothing wrong. She proclaimed that federal authorities and vigilantes were the criminals because they tried "to make foreigners accept the Declaration of Independence and the Constitution at the point of a club" without telling them "the guarantees of freedom and liberty and independence contained in the Constitution." Goldman defiantly stated that she had been an anarchist for thirty years and expected to die one. "If that is a crime," she declared, "help yourself to your method of punishment." She denied, however, that she had induced anyone to kill, rob, or destroy. She claimed she only stated her opinion, which the Constitution gave her every right to do. Finally, Goldman demonstrated she had gained confidence in her impact since her contemplative fiftieth birthday at the Missouri prison. She averred that her time in America had not been in vain because she helped mold the intellectual life of the American people. "I assure you if I had my thirty-four years to live over in the United States, I should be glad to do the same things, over and over again," she said.[28]

Goldman received word on December 3 that she would be deported. The deportation order indicated that Goldman had violated the Immigration Acts of 1917 and 1918 because she was an alien anarchist who advocated for overthrowing government and "all forms of law" by force or violence and she had counseled others to assassinate public officials.[29] Weinberger petitioned the U.S. District Court of the Southern District of New York for a writ of habeas corpus, insisting that Goldman was a legal citizen, immigration officials had hastened her hearing so proper documentation could not be secured, and the government was violating her liberty by detaining her at Ellis Island.[30] Federal authorities maintained that Goldman was an alien anarchist, and Judge Julius Mayer, who had presided over Goldman's federal court trial, dismissed the writ.[31] In Weinberger's request for a Supreme Court appeal, he argued that the "Anarchy Deportation Laws" of 1917 and 1918 were unconstitutional in respect to the First Amendment, "in that the holding of mere opinions, whether of anarchism or any other belief, religious, political or social, can not [*sic*] be made the basis for a warrant of deportation."[32] Though Justice Louis Brandeis granted Goldman an appeal, she chose to return to Russia with Berkman rather than stay on her own and raise funds for an appeal she believed she would lose.[33]

As ordered, Goldman and Berkman surrendered themselves on December 5 to immigration officials at Ellis Island, where they were photographed and finger printed "like convicted criminals."[34] In a pamphlet penned while they awaited their transport to Russia, the pair proclaimed that all of the Russian refugees detained at Ellis Island were treated like felons. Many had been beaten and tortured before being "thrust into the bull pens of Ellis Island," separated from their families. Any who protested against their isolation and "the putrid food" were "placed in the insane asylum." Many had resorted to hunger strikes.[35]

The pamphlet was Berkman and Goldman's parting shot at America's sham of a democracy. They penned the tract in secret; Berkman smuggled the manuscript out for publication through a friend.[36] Robert Minor, an American-born radical cartoonist and frequent contributor to *Mother Earth*, wrote an introductory note. He averred that although Berkman and Goldman were deported as Russians, they were "the best of Americans" because they "fought for the elementary rights of men here in our country when others were afraid to speak, or would not pay the price."[37] Berkman and Goldman's

Figure 5.2 Goldman's deportation photograph at Ellis Island, December 1919. Source: Library of Congress.

message began with familiar refrains against war, its capitalist origins, and the intolerance of dissent it spawned. They pronounced liberty and free speech to be dead. The authors chastised Americans for allowing their representatives to enact suppressive legislation, under the auspices of war necessity, that would continue prohibiting unapproved thoughts and views in peace time. "The practice of stifling and choking free speech and press, established and tolerated during the war, sets a most dangerous precedent for after-war days," Berkman and Goldman asserted. "The principle of such outrages upon liberty once introduced, it will require a long and arduous struggle to win back the liberties lost."[38] Americans had been too well swayed by war propaganda, Berkman and Goldman argued. The campaign filled the country with hatred, intolerance, persecution, and suppression, and with the war over and German relations restored, the hatred had to be channeled somewhere else. Americans chose the "Bolshevik menace" that "threatened rich men of this free country" because the "press, the pulpit, all the servile tools of capitalism and imperialism combine to paint Russia, Soviet Russia, in colors of blood and infamy." The press, Berkman and Goldman declared, had turned good Americans into "bestial mobs" against the " 'foreigner,' whose sole crime consists in taking seriously the American guarantees of free speech, free press, and free assembly."[39] The pamphlet concluded that America's labor force must rise up against suppression of free thought and speech. "Only your united effort can conquer the peril that menaces you," Berkman and Goldman encouraged. "Take action."[40]

On December 21, 1919, Goldman and 248 other alleged anarchists departed for Finland on the *Buford*, also known as the "Red Ark"; from there, a train took the deportees to Russia. Nearly 200 of the ship's passengers were Russian workers apprehended in the November Palmer raids; another 43 were anarchists like Goldman and Berkman who had been captured earlier.[41] Only three of the deportees were female. Goldman shared quarters with two women from the Union of Russian Workers: Dora Lipkin and Ethel Bernstein, who had come to the United States as a child and had no memory of Russia or its language.[42] The Red Ark's departure was nothing like Goldman's arrival in 1885. The passengers had been hastily awakened and rushed onto the ship in the middle of the night. From her cabin below deck, Goldman felt the boat lurch into the harbor at 4:20 a.m., and—as she thought of her countrymen exiled to Siberia from Czarist Russia—she ironically caught a glimpse of the Statue of Liberty through a small porthole.[43]

When Goldman arrived at Ellis Island earlier that month, a reporter commented, "That is the end, Emma Goldman, isn't it?" Goldman replied, "It may only be the beginning."[44] In many senses, it was a beginning. First, the mass deportation marked for the American press the beginning of a process they long had been calling for. Newspapers celebrated the departure of Goldman and others of her ilk, calling for more ships to cart off even larger cargoes of un-Americans in the future.[45] The government answered with more raids as the Red Scare lasted well into 1920.[46] Second, Goldman's deportation marked the

Figure 5.3 Holding immigrants in pens was not a new practice in 1919. This image depicts pens at Ellis Island in 1906.

Source: Library of Congress.

start of a new chapter in her anarchist crusade. She remained active in anarchist causes until her death in 1940, lecturing around Europe and Canada. She was particularly proud to support anarcho-syndicalists during the Spanish Civil War of the 1930s.[47] Third, and most importantly for this book, though Goldman lost her free speech battles in the

United States, her struggles lit a spark that led to greater consideration of First Amendment protections in future Supreme Court trials.

Goldman's Legacy

Scholars often identify the Espionage Act of 1917 as the catalyst or instigating factor that ultimately led the Supreme Court to squarely address the meaning of First Amendment safeguards for freedom of expression.[48] Essentially, historians have contended that the sweeping language and enthusiastic use of the law by government officials to halt dissent caused Americans to question, for the first time in the nation's history, the powers of the government to limit expression. Legal scholar David Rabban explained, "The extensive repression of antiwar and radical speech during and after World War I made many Americans sensitive to infringements on speech for the first time."[49] Such a conclusion is further supported by the fact that the first wave of cases in which the Supreme Court addressed the First Amendment dealt with the constitutionality of the Espionage Act.[50] For this reason, Charles Schenck, who was arrested in August 1917 alongside Elizabeth Baer for handing out anti-draft leaflets in Philadelphia, is generally recognized as the person associated with the beginnings of First Amendment jurisprudence in the United States. After all, almost any communication law course begins with *Schenck v. United States*. Of course, by the time Schenck was arrested, Goldman was already in a Missouri prison. Her appeal before the Supreme Court in December 1917, as Schenck and Baer were being convicted for violating the Espionage Act in a federal district courtroom less than a hundred miles away in Pennsylvania, has traditionally been ignored or forgotten in First Amendment history.

This book contends that this oversight is a mistake. Goldman's life, the coverage of her trial, and the timing and outcomes of her appeals in 1917 require that her name be included alongside those of Schenck, Eugene Debs, and Jacob Abrams when we consider the origins of how we understand the emergence of free expression rights in the United States. While Goldman's experiences do not include being the instigator involved in the first landmark freedom-of-expression case, as Schenck's do, or the person whose appeal before the Supreme Court led to the creation of the marketplace of ideas theory of the First Amendment, as Abrams's does, she can claim two important distinctions that they and their brethren cannot. First, Goldman's appeal before the Supreme Court in 1917 was the last instance when justices, despite facing a clear First Amendment question, avoided considering the matter as a freedom of expression concern. Second, her trial in federal district court led to one of the first instances when freedom of expression was placed squarely before a national audience as editorials, columns, and letters to the editor discussed the values and limitations that should be associated with freedom of speech.

Legal Legacy

As the better-known *Schenck* and *Abrams* cases made their way through the court system, Goldman's appeal was always ahead of theirs. When Justice Oliver Wendell Holmes conveyed the Supreme Court's reasoning in its decision to uphold Schenck's conviction in 1919, he called upon *Goldman v. United States*, from the previous term, as one of only four cases he used to support his argument regarding the limitations that surround freedom of expression.[51] Justice Holmes indicated that, in light of the Court's failure to address freedom of expression in *Goldman*, he was endeavoring to clarify that position in *Schenck*. He reasoned in the opinion that Goldman's "case might be said to dispose of the present contention if the precedent covers all media concludendi. But as the right to free speech was not referred to specially, we have thought fit to add a few words."[52] Such an inclusion in the first true free-expression case in the Court's history would appear to be quite an accomplishment for a decision that did not include a single reference to the First Amendment or freedom of expression.[53] It furthermore provides evidence that Justice Holmes, to some extent, understood Goldman's case, despite its lack of explicit attention to the First Amendment, as dealing with freedom of expression concerns.

Importantly, the Supreme Court has cited its decision in *Goldman* on several other occasions, including in *Dennis v. United States*, a crucial case from 1951 regarding how the nation should deal with seditious speech. Eugene Dennis, the general secretary of the Communist Party in the United States, was convicted of advocating the overthrow of the government. In citing *Goldman*, Chief Justice Fred Vinson found support for the conclusion that a person's words can be sufficient for a conviction. In other words, no physical impediment of the draft was required for the court to rule in favor of limiting Goldman's expression.[54] Similarly, Dennis did not physically attempt to overthrow the government, he only spoke about the subject. Speaking about it was sufficient for the Court, with a little help from the reasoning found in *Goldman*, to uphold Dennis's conviction.

These instances are not the only times that Goldman's World War I-era struggles in American courts found their way into First Amendment discussions during this time period. After justices ruled in the *Schenck*, *Debs*, and *Frohwerk* cases in spring 1919, Zechariah Chafee, a Harvard Law School professor and friend of Justice Holmes, published "Freedom of Speech in War Time," which over time has become a landmark discussion of freedom of expression.[55] The article, published in the June 1919

Harvard Law Review, discusses Judge Julius Meyer's understandings of freedom of speech from Goldman's district-court trial. Similarly, Judge Learned Hand, another friend of Justice Holmes's, discussed Goldman's plight in his ruling in *Masses v. Patten* on July 24, 1917, only weeks after her conviction. In that case, postal officials, citing the Espionage Act, refused to mail copies of the socialist magazine, *The Masses*.[56] Judge Hand ruled in favor of the magazine, which included a poem about the recently convicted Goldman. Judge Hand concluded that, "Let us give them every chance for acquittal that the constitution of the times allow. Let us give them every chance to state their faith."[57] On appeal in the Second Circuit in November 1917, the judges were not quite as sympathetic to the magazine's concerns and overturned Hand's ruling.[58] That is not the point, however. Crucially, we see Goldman's struggle in federal courts—courts that paid little or no attention to First Amendment concerns before and during her trial—immediately showing up in crucial considerations regarding freedom of expression.

Chafee incorporated Hand's reasoning from *Masses* into his article "Freedom of Speech in War Time," concluding that "there is no finer statement of the right of free speech than these words."[59] Justice Holmes read Chafee's article and, according to Rabban, was significantly influenced by its reasoning.[60] Despite the impact the article might have had, Justice Holmes disagreed with Chafee's assessment of Judge Hand's ruling in the *Masses* case. Justice Holmes expressed this same opinion directly to Judge Hand in a letter in February 1919, which was written during the same period that he was composing the Supreme Court's opinions for *Schenck*, *Debs*, and *Frohwerk*.[61] Thus, Goldman's legal struggles in 1917 were incorporated into crucial legal and scholarly discussions regarding freedom of expression, particularly as the Supreme Court prepared to rule in the landmark *Schenck* and *Abrams* cases in 1919.

Print Legacy

Before Goldman's struggles in the courtroom drew leading legal minds such as Justice Holmes, Judge Hand, and Chafee to consider the boundaries of freedom of expression in legal opinions and law journals, her trial in a New York federal district court in June and July 1917 spurred editorial boards, columnists, and letter-to-the-editor writers to engage in discourse about freedom of expression. The discussion consistently considered Goldman's identity, evaluating where she was from, what her beliefs were, and how well she and her comrade Berkman adhered to the tenets of civic nationalism. An editorial in the *San Diego Evening News* emphasized that "neither of these blatant disturbers of our peace is an American citizen."[62] The *Philadelphia Inquirer*, similarly, found that

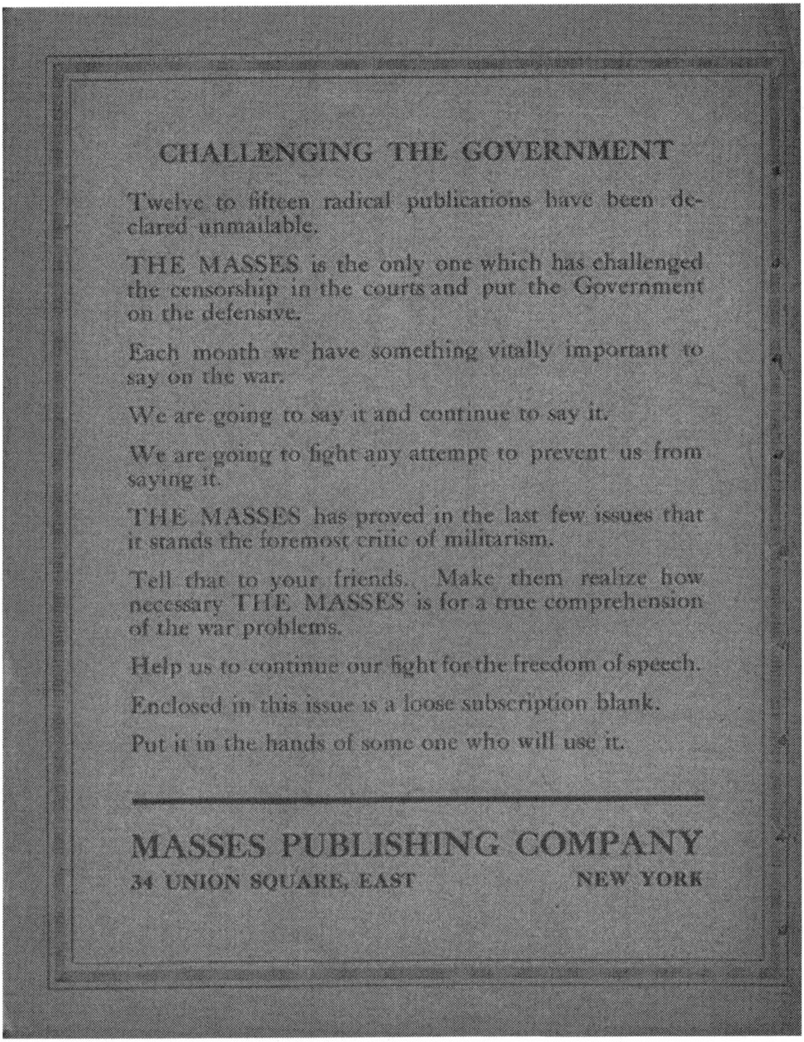

CHALLENGING THE GOVERNMENT

Twelve to fifteen radical publications have been declared unmailable.

THE MASSES is the only one which has challenged the censorship in the courts and put the Government on the defensive.

Each month we have something vitally important to say on the war.

We are going to say it and continue to say it.

We are going to fight any attempt to prevent us from saying it.

THE MASSES has proved in the last few issues that it stands the foremost critic of militarism.

Tell that to your friends. Make them realize how necessary THE MASSES is for a true comprehension of the war problems.

Help us to continue our fight for the freedom of speech.

Enclosed in this issue is a loose subscription blank.

Put it in the hands of some one who will use it.

MASSES PUBLISHING COMPANY

34 UNION SQUARE, EAST NEW YORK

Figure 5.4 The back cover of *The Masses* September 1917 issue discussed the magazine's legal challenge of government censorship.

Source: Tamiment Library and Robert F. Wagner Labor Archives, New York University.

"the criminal aliens should go the way of deportation. There is no room in a free country for such miserable creatures."[63] The *Oregonian* editorial board concluded that "it is impossible for a mind and spirit like the Goldman woman's to be harmonized with any scheme of government or any rule of life. She is an outlaw, temperamentally, intellectually and morally."[64] Thus, newspaper audiences encountered discussions about Goldman's rights that were based upon her status as an immigrant and the level to which she, according to the authors, aligned with American ideals. Reverberating through these and other instances were themes of otherness, where her perspectives were discounted because she was understood as someone who did not share American values.

The discussion that took place in newspapers also considered the boundaries of freedom of expression more specifically, particularly during wartime. A letter to the editor in the *Salt Lake Tribune* contended that "the time has come for treasonable editors and orators to shut up or be locked up."[65] The *Dallas Morning News* published a similar sentiment, stating that, whether they are guilty of a crime or not, they should be imprisoned because "the country cannot well afford to be distracted and annoyed by them."[66] Similarly, another letter-writer concluded that "Emma Goldman was not sent to prison for speaking freely, but because her words were seditiously calculated to impair confidence in the government."[67] Thus, in these types of pieces, audiences encountered arguments that expression that threatens the government or its interests should be limited. An editorial in the *Belleville Democrat* echoed these conclusions, finding that "the right of free speech … there is no such thing." The piece concluded, "To oppose the government in wartime is treason and treason is a crime."[68]

The entire editorial debate, which unfolded before and during Goldman's trial in June and July of 1917, was followed by Schenck and Baer's arrest in Pennsylvania, the arrests of Emmanuel Baltzer and dozens more German-American farmers in South Dakota, and Jacob Abrams and other Russian immigrants' arrests in New York during the next month. While Goldman's free expression legacy cannot be identified in the same terms as *Schenck* and *Abrams*, it also cannot be ignored.

Notes

1 "Trial and Speeches of Alexander Berkman and Emma Goldman in the United States in District Court, in the City of New York, July 1917" (New York: Mother Earth Publishing Association, 1917), 73–74, in Candace Falk, with Ronald J. Zboray, et al., eds., *The Emma Goldman Papers: A Microfilm Edition* (Alexandria, VA: Chadwyck-Healey, Inc., 1990; hereafter referred to as Goldman Papers), reel 57.

2 Goldman spent two weeks in prison after the federal court trial but was released on $25,000 bail pending appeal. Berkman was released but extradited to California for trial on a separate offense, for which he was acquitted. Emma Goldman, *Living My Life* (Garden City, NY: Garden City Publishing, 1934), 624–637; Emma Goldman, "Between Jails," *Mother* Earth, August 1917, 207–212; Emma Goldman, "Dear Friends," August 1, 1917, Goldman Papers, reel 57. Several court documents regarding Goldman's release on bail also can be found in Goldman Papers, reel 57.

3 Leonard Abbott, "The War Hysteria and Our Protest," *Mother Earth*, August 1917, 202–206; Goldman, "Between Jails," 208.

4 Memos from Postal Solicitor W. H. Lamar to the New Jersey and New York Postmasters, both dated September 11, 1917, declared the August issue unmailable and directed the postmasters to destroy all copies. A letter from the same date from Lamar to Assistant Postmaster General A. M. Dockery suggested that steps be taken to permanently withdraw the magazine's mailing privileges. Dockery summoned the publishers of *Mother Earth* to defend their worthiness for mailing privileges in a letter dated September 12, 1917; Goldman Papers, reel 59.

5 Goldman, *Living My Life*, 642.

6 Emma Goldman, "Dear Friend," September 28, 1917, Goldman Papers, reel 10.

7 *Mother Earth Bulletin*, October 1917.

8 Ben L. Reitman to the Postmaster, September 22, 1917, in *Mother Earth Bulletin*, October 1917. For an examination of the Espionage Act's constitutionality, see Geoffrey R. Stone, "Judge Learned Hand and the Espionage Act of 1917: A Mystery Unraveled," *University of Chicago Law Review* 70, 1 (2003): 335–358.

9 Numerous memos in Goldman Papers reels 59–62 demonstrate that postal officials scrutinized the *Bulletin* from the beginning, noting objectionable material and occasionally excluding issues on a case-by-case basis. See also Comyn's mimeographed "Instead of a Magazine," dated June 29, 1918, Goldman Papers, reel 61.

10 Robert Bowen to Frederick Mulker, July 10, 1918, Goldman Papers, reel 61.

11 See, for example, Emma Goldman, "The Russian Revolution," *Mother Earth Bulletin*, December 1917, 1–2; Emma Goldman, "The Great Hope," *Mother Earth Bulletin*, January 1918, 2–3; Emma Goldman, "On the Way to Golgotha," *Mother Earth Bulletin*, February 1918, 1.

12 Goldman, *Living My Life*, 688.

13 For several memos noting specific correspondence held as suspicious, see Goldman Papers, reels 60–63.

14 Emma Goldman to W. S. Van Valkenburgh, October 19, 1917, Goldman Papers, reel 11; Goldman, "Between Jails," 209; Emma Goldman, "Farewell, Friends and Comrades!" *Mother Earth Bulletin*, January 1918, 1.

15 Bonnie Stepenoff, "Mother and Teacher as Missouri State Penitentiary Inmates: Goldman and O'Hare, 1917–1920," *Missouri Historical Review* 85, 4 (1991): 409.

16 Goldman, *Living My Life*, 686.

17 J. Edgar Hoover, "Memorandum for Mr. Creighton," August 23, 1919, Goldman Papers, reel 63.

18 Warrant for the Arrest of Emma Goldman, U.S. Department of Labor, September 5, 1919, and Henry Weinberger to John W. Abercrombie, September 11, 1919, both in Goldman Papers, reel 63. Authorities had called for a deportation warrant as Goldman awaited her Supreme Court appeal in July 1917, but Assistant Secretary of Labor Louis Post refused to sign it because of lack of proof that Goldman was an alien; see Louis Post memo to Anthony Caminetti, July 21, 1917, Goldman Papers, reel 57.

19 Report on Emma Goldman, Bureau of Investigation, Department of Justice, September 19, 1919, Goldman Papers, reel 63; Goldman, *Living My Life*, 18–25; Alexander Berkman and Emma Goldman, "Deportation: Its Meaning and Menace" (New York: Ellis Island, December 1919), 20. Kershner's status was not a secret to Goldman at the time of her deportation; newspapers reported the ruling in 1908, gloating that officials easily could deport her then. See, for example, "Emma Goldman Loses Rights," *Detroit Free Press*, April 9, 1909; "Emma Goldman Can Be Deported," *Buffalo Evening News*, April 8, 1908; "Emma Goldman Ready to Fight Deportation," *Los Angeles Herald*, April 10, 1909.

20 "Why Delay Deportations?", *Minneapolis Journal*, reprinted in *Argus-Leader* (Sioux Falls, SD), October 30, 1919.

21 "No Room for Anarchists," *Ohio State Journal* (Columbus, OH), reprinted in *Lincoln* (NE) *Journal Star*, October 30, 1919.

22 The transcript of her deportation hearing lists all of the exhibits read into the record; see Deportation Hearing of Emma Goldman (transcript), Bureau of Investigation, Department of Labor, Ellis Island, New York, October 27 and November 12, 1919, Goldman Papers, reel 63.

23 Goldman, *Living My Life*, 704.

24 Ibid., 708.

25 Berkman and Goldman, "Deportation," 8.

26 Goldman, *Living My Life*, 709.

27 Emma Goldman, "Speech on Political Deportations" (speech, Detroit, MI, November 26, 1919), Goldman Papers, reel 64.

28 Ibid.

29 John W. Abercrombie to the Acting Commissioner of Immigration, Ellis Island, December 1, 1919, Goldman Papers, reel 64.

30 Weinberger claimed the court that canceled Kershner's citizenship did not have the authority do so. *United States ex rel Goldman v. Caminetti*: Petition for Writ of Habeas Corpus, December 5, 1919, Goldman Papers, reel 64.

31 *United States ex rel Goldman v. Caminetti*: Stenographer's Notes, December 8, 1919, and Order Dismissing Writ of Habeas Corpus, December 9, 1919, Goldman Papers, reel 64.

32 *United States ex rel Goldman v. Caminetti*: Assignment of Errors, December 10, 1919, Goldman Papers, reel 64.

33 Goldman, *Living My Life*, 712–714; *United States ex rel Goldman v. Caminetti*: Allowance of Appeal, December 10, 1919, Goldman Papers, reel 64. Berkman's fate already was decided, following a deportation hearing in Atlanta upon his prison release in September.

34 Goldman, *Living My Life*, 715.

35 Berkman and Goldman, "Deportation," 18.

36 Goldman, *Living My Life*, 713.

37 Berkman and Goldman, "Deportation," 3. The last page of the pamphlet indicates that copies could be purchased from M. E. Fitzgerald (Berkman's lover Eleanor) at 857 Broadway, New York City.

38 Ibid., 8.

39 Ibid., 10, 12–14.

40 Ibid., 24.

41 The remaining passengers had violated other aspects of the immigration acts; see Robert K. Murray, *Red Scare: A Study in National Hysteria, 1919–1920* (Minneapolis: University of Minnesota Press, 1955), 207.
42 Goldman, *Living My Life*, 715.
43 Ibid., 717.
44 Ibid., 709–710.
45 The *New York Tribune* of December 22, 1919 carried multiple stories on the *Buford*'s sailing spanning two pages, with several mentions of Goldman and Berkman. See also "Let More Deportations Follow," *Philadelphia Inquirer*, December 23, 1919; "Soviet Ark On High Seas Russia Bound," *Buffalo Evening Times*, December 22, 1919; "Anarchist Ark Leaves Country With Alien Reds," *Times-Leader* (Wilkes-Barre, PA), December 23, 1919.
46 Murray, *Red Scare*.
47 See Mikhail Bjorge, "'They Shall Not Die!': Anarchists, Syndicalists, Communists, and the Sacco and Vanzetti Solidarity Campaign in Canada," *Labour/Le Travail* 75 (Spring 2015): 43–73; Goldman, *Living My Life*, 726–993; Emma Goldman, *My Disillusionment in Russia* (New York: Thomas Y. Crowell Company, 1970); Theresa Moritz and Albert Moritz, *The World's Most Dangerous Woman: A New Biography of Emma Goldman* (Vancouver: Subway Books, 2002); David Porter, *Vision on Fire: Emma Goldman on the Spanish Revolution* (Chico, CA: AK Press, 2006); Kenneth C. Wenzer, *Anarchists Adrift: Emma Goldman and Alexander Berkman* (St. James, NY: Brandywine Press, 1996); Alice Wexler, *Emma Goldman in Exile* (Boston: Beacon Press, 1989); Martin Zeilig, "Emma Goldman in Winnipeg," *Manitoba History* 25 (Spring 1993): 23–27.
48 David M. Rabban, *Free Speech in the Forgotten Years* (Cambridge: Cambridge University Press, 1997), 16–20; Donald Johnson, "Wilson, Burleson, and Censorship in the First World War," *The Journal of Southern History* 28, 1 (1962): 46–48; Sam Lebovic, *Free Speech and Unfree News* (Cambridge: Harvard University Press, 2016), 16–17.
49 Rabban, *Free Speech in the Forgotten Years*, 16.
50 See *Schenck v. United States*, 249 U.S. 47 (1919); *Debs v. United States*, 249 U.S. 211 (1919); *Frohwerk v. United States*, 249 U.S. 204 (1919); *Abrams v. United States*, 250 U.S. 616 (1919).
51 *Schenck*, 249 U.S. at 52.
52 Ibid.
53 See *Goldman v. United States*, 245 U.S. 474 (1918).
54 *Dennis v. United States*, 341 U.S. 494, 503–504 (1951).
55 Zechariah Chafee, "Freedom Speech in War Time," *Harvard Law Review* 32, 8 (1919).
56 *Masses v. Patten*, 244 F. 535, 545 (S.D.N.Y., 1917).
57 Ibid.
58 *Masses v. Patten*, 246 F. 24 (2d cir., 1917).
59 Chafee, "Freedom of Speech in War Time," 962.
60 Rabban, *Free Speech in the Forgotten Years*, 7.
61 Oliver Wendell Holmes to Learned Hand, February 25, 1919, Oliver Wendell Holmes Jr. Digital Suite, Harvard Law Library.
62 "Jailed 'Philosophers'," *San Diego Evening News*, July 11, 1917.

63 "To Jail With the Anarchists," *Philadelphia Inquirer*, July 11, 1917.
64 "Fair Warning," *Oregonian*, July 11, 1917.
65 "Shut Up or be Locked Up," *Salt Lake Telegram*, July 2, 1917.
66 *Dallas Morning News*, June 28, 1917.
67 "The Fate of Emma Goldman," *San Jose Mercury News*, July 11, 1917.
68 "Pathological Troublemakers and Copperheads Must Go To Prison," *Belleville Democrat*, July 10, 1917.

Index

Taylor & Francis Group
an informa business

Taylor & Francis eBooks

www.taylorfrancis.com

A single destination for eBooks from Taylor & Francis with increased functionality and an improved user experience to meet the needs of our customers.

90,000+ eBooks of award-winning academic content in Humanities, Social Science, Science, Technology, Engineering, and Medical written by a global network of editors and authors.

TAYLOR & FRANCIS EBOOKS OFFERS:

- A streamlined experience for our library customers
- A single point of discovery for all of our eBook content
- Improved search and discovery of content at both book and chapter level

REQUEST A FREE TRIAL

support@taylorfrancis.com

Routledge
Taylor & Francis Group

CRC Press
Taylor & Francis Group